\*   \*   \*

**L. U. CIPHER, Jr.** *is an enigmatic author about whom nothing is known except that he is from an old family with deep roots in and below the Hell's Kitchen neighborhood of Manhattan.*

**JOHN NASSIVERA** *is a former resident of Manhattan's Hell's Kitchen neighborhood. He is a retired professor and a Life Fellow of Columbia University's Society of Fellows in the Humanities. He received his doctorate from McGill University, but he's not the kind of doctor that does anyone any good. Upon discovering this manuscript he became so troubled by its contents that he became a Roman Catholic and retreated to the Green Mountains of Vermont, where he lives quietly with his family and enjoys breakfasts with his parish priest. His next book will be out in 2011 and is titled "GOD IS GREAT: Confessions of a Former Secular Humanist."*

\*   \*   \*

# THE DEVIL'S DICTIONARY

## FOR AN UNGODLY AGE

THE WORDS YOU NEED FOR TODAY'S BLASPHEMOUS,
SCATOLOGICAL, BUT POLITICALLY CORRECT WORLD

compiled by
**L. U. CIPHER, Jr.**

abridged & edited by
**JOHN NASSIVERA**

PANDEMONIUM PUBLISHERS
*a division of*
NATAS INTERNATIONAL GROUP

*Omnis obstat.*

*Imprimatur:*  Least Rev. Demonio Negroponte, S.O.L.
Sub-Bishop of Salem, Massachusetts, USA


*The* Omnis Obstat *and* Imprimatur *are official declarations that a book contains doctrinal and moral error. The implication is that those who granted the* Omnis Obstat *and* Imprimatur *agree wholeheartedly with the blasphemous and scandalous statements expressed.*

Pandemonium Publishers
*Natas International Group*
New York, NY

Author's representative for all rights queries:
SUSAN SCHULMAN LITERARY AGENCY
Ms. Susan Schulman
454 West 44th Street
New York, NY  10036
212-713-1633
Schulman@aol.com


ISBN  978-1-453-86982-6

Cover Design by Drew Ann Dunigan.

**Available for purchase from:**
**AMAZON.COM  (paperback)**
**also via KINDLE  (e-book)**

*This book*
*is dedicated*
*Screwtape, Wormwood,*
*& all Gangs of Virtue.*

*-- L. U. C.*

# EDITOR'S PREFACE

In the middle of the journey of my life I found myself lost in a dark subway station somewhere beneath Times Square in New York City, wandering in a subterranean warren of somewhat foreboding tunnels. I had somehow managed, lost in thought, to take a very wrong turn. I must have passed signs that clearly said, "Do not enter," or "Abandon all hope, you who enter here."

I had gone down a couple flights to lower levels of tracks, to a platform that had not seen a train in many, many years. The dull and rusted tracks, some five feet below the platform, had a little stream of dirty water flowing down between them. I thought, just for a moment, that perhaps it was the origin of the River Styx.

Then I saw it.

Down at the far end of the abandoned platform I saw what appeared to be a rather high-end red leather suitcase. It was quite large—and this part was very strange—the abundant dust and dirt all around had not settled on it. It looked like it had been sitting there only a short time. Stranger still, there were no footprints in the dust on the platform around it. How it got there I shall never know.

Of course, I had to open it. Inside I found pages and pages of some sort of manuscript, written in a striking, old fashioned handwriting, but cramped and angular—one could almost say in an angry hand. The pages were not in any particular order. In fact, I only found the title page and dedication later, shuffled into the middle of the chaotic pile. I remember also that upon opening the suitcase there was a distinct odor of sulfur.

I found my way back to the surface, bringing the suitcase with me. I managed to carry the it down the sidewalk and over to my apartment building on the corner of 43$^{rd}$ Street and 11$^{th}$ Avenue. What you now have in your hands in this little book is a small sample of some of the pages I found in that suitcase. I have collected them and put them in alphabetical order. I have edited the writing as little as possible, *and please remember that the points of view expressed are not my own—I am merely the editor.*

Of course, I found the writings in these manuscript pages very disturbing.

To this day I do not know whether they are the ravings of a madman or whether they indeed have some diabolical origin. Either way, as highly offensive as much of it is, at the same time the material can strike a little too close to the bone and can have a certain ring of menacing truth about it.

I hope you will find this strange text as interesting and worrisome as I have.

*--- J. N.*

---

*Note:* *In the manuscript's text, the words "Our Father Below" and "Our Father" are used frequently. Even though the use of these forms of address may seem offensive and even blasphemous, I have thought it best to preserve the original wording.*

# THE DEVIL'S DICTIONARY
## For an Ungodly Age

# A

**Abel,** *proper noun/name.* The bad brother. (See *Cain.*)

**Abortion,** *noun.* An effective and highly reliable form of birth control, protected by law in enlightened democracies, usage of which has happily been increasing greatly since the late 20th century. Yes, it may be controversial in some circles, but nothing is perfect. We are pleased to note that in more and more developed countries abortions now outnumber live births by growing margins.

**Abraham (Abrahamic Religions),** *proper noun.* Abraham was the unfortunate fellow through whom God started all the trouble, somewhere around 2000 B. C. It was to Abraham that God promised the land of Israel. It was Abraham whom God's angel stopped from performing a pagan-inspired human sacrifice of his son, Isaac, on a large rock atop a hill in the place that became Jerusalem—the location of the First and Second Temple of the Jews and since the 7th century the location of the Muslim shrine known as the Dome of the Rock. It was through the descendants of Abraham, via his sons Isaac and Ishmael, that the planet has been plagued or blessed (depending on one's bias) with the religions of Judaism, Christianity, and Islam.

**Abscond,** *verb.* To leave in a mysterious and quiet way, often taking along with you something of great importance to some one else. As in, for example, God made the world (not very well), saw the mess it was in, and then he *absconded,* taking his promise to help along with him and leaving poor humans to fix things on their own. We faithful servants of Our Father Below are fond of the Latin name for this God, *Deus Absconditus.* Enlightened people who believe in this sort of God call themselves Diests. Fortunately for the United States, a number of the writers of the U.S. constitution were card-carrying Diests, so they made sure that the word "God" did not appear in the document—creating a loophole large enough to drive a truck through. But that wasn't their *original intent,* after all they didn't have trucks then. (See *Deus Absconditus* and *Original Intent.*)

**Abstinence,** *noun.* A concept born out of the dangerously misinformed idea that humans are capable of refraining from anything. The best and most sensible way to handle temptation is to give in to it.

**Academe,** *noun.* A simple, public grove in ancient Athens where various forms of sophistry were taught, corrupting naïve and impressionable youth. (See *Socrates, Sophistry.*)

**Academic Institution,** *noun.* An complex of expensive buildings called a *campus* in the modern world where various forms of sophistry are taught, corrupting naïve and impressionable youth. (See *Campus, Socrates, Sophistry.*)

**Academic Freedom,** *noun.* The freedom of college professors to be and say exactly what their colleagues and administration require that they be and say.

**Academic Question,** *noun.* A pointless question that may or may not have an answer, but if it does, the answer will be equally pointless. This type of question is the primary focus of academics.

**Actress,** *noun.* A sexist, politically incorrect term for a female actor.

***Ad Nauseam,*** *Latin expression.* The length of time life goes on—unless one *carpe diems** the living hell out of it. (**seize the day*)

**Adoption,** *noun.*   An out-dated legal procedure whereby a husband and wife would take on the duties of becoming a child's permanent parents. Now with the modern medical procedures of artificial insemination, in vitro fertilization, and surrogate motherhood *adoption* is no longer preferred or necessary.

**Adultery,** *noun.*   The penultimate stage of marriage.  (See *Divorce.*)

**Advertise, Advertising,** *verb and noun.*   The art and craft of manufacturing desire; a most sublime activity, brought to new heights in the 20th century, that convinces people to crave things and services they do not need by spending money they do not have in order to find happiness they will not achieve.

**Afterlife,** *noun.*   Christians and Muslims believe in heaven.   Atheists believe in worms.   Nobody believes in hell anymore.  Most are in for a surprise.

**Agnostic,** *noun.*   Some one who hasn't bothered to make up his mind yet about the most important question haunting human existence.  But sooner or later he will.

**Alcoholic,** *noun.* A person who has received the revelation of truth that the only spirits within human reach are conveniently packaged in a bottle.

**Alien Abduction,** *noun.* In the United States, a round-up of illegal immigrant laborers and their deportation back to Mexico. *Alien Abductions* are very rare occurrences because if they happened with regular frequency a whole swath of the American economy would be brought to its knees.

**Alien Life Form,** *noun.* A corporation. United States law says a corporation is a person; all right, but enter into the record that a corporate person is an *Alien Life Form* and a natural (or rather, unnatural) predator of human persons. No other *Alien Life Forms* have been discovered on planet earth—specifically none from outer space.

**Alienation,** *noun.* The natural and perennial psychological condition of humankind in Western, Post-Modern society. (See *Psychotropic Drugs.*)

**Allah,** *proper noun.* See God. And that's the problem.

**Alone,** *adjective.* In good company.

**Altruism,** *noun.* A mental disorder marked by an unhealthy concern for the welfare of others.

**Ambition,** *noun.* Should creep close to the ground and stay out of the light.

**Ambrose Bierce,** *author.* An American writer of the late 19th and early 20th century. He wrote a well known book unfortunately known as *The Devil's Dictionary,* which was created without any consultation or permission from those who work with and represent Our Father Below.

**American Bar Association,** *proper noun.* No comment. We plead the fifth.

**Amoral, Immoral,** *adjective.* There is an important and fine distinction here: An *Amoral* person or act is one that is without moral quality, neither moral nor immoral; whereas an *Immoral* person or act is one that is specifically counter to a particular social or personal system of ethics. Granted, they amount to the same thing in the end; however, being *Amoral* is more subtle and subversive, so consequently is more effective and less apt to be obstructed. For example, corporations and stock markets are *Amoral* in as much as they are neither moral nor immoral. Yes, a corporation under U. S. law is a person; however, corporate persons are not required or expected to possess personal morality, which is why corporate persons are far more powerful, useful, influential, and superior in every way to human persons, who are required to refrain from being *Amoral* or *Immoral.*

**Amusement,** *noun.* The best *Amusement* is the one that is the most pointless.

**Anger,** *noun.* Is the sinew of the soul.

**Anger Management,** *noun & psychological term.* Why would anyone want to?

**Anglican Church** (aka **Church of England, Episcopal Church),** *proper noun.* A Christian denomination founded by an unscrupulous man and murderer (King Henry VIII) who wanted to divorce his wife and have sex and children with a different woman in order to further his unbridled power and royal dynasty—while at the same time establishing his own national church with himself as the head. To this day, the King or Queen of England is still the head of the Church of England/Anglican Church. True to its origins, this denomination is now widely known for its ordination of single and/or married, and/or divorced, and/or paramour, and/or single and pregnant priests, without regard to gender, gender preference or identification, race, religion, national origin, marital or parental status, etc, etc., etc. A going concern in more ways than one, currently about 1.7 % (1, *point, 7, that's not a typo*) of England's population are church-going members of the Anglican Church. Of this 1.7 %, a significant number are now returning to the Catholic Church—the very same church that old King Henry did his very best to shut down and stamp out. God works in mysterious ways.

**Anglosphere,** *noun.* The ever growing realm on the planet, in the sky, and in space where English language and culture—i.e., American culture—is the dominant force.

**Angst,** *noun.* A comforting feeling derived from dread, anxiety, and anguish.

**Animal Instinct,** *noun.* Humans are part of the animal kingdom and yet a certain percentage of them persist in believing that they can rise above *Animal Instinct.* Fortunately this unenlightened percentage is growing smaller and smaller.

**Anthropic Principle,** *noun.* This is a 20th century term of theoretical physics and cosmology, used to refer to the discovery in these fields that the

universe seems to have been specifically constructed in such a way as to allow for human
intelligence to arise or, in different phrasing, the
universe seems to have known all along that a
human-like intelligence was coming. This is an
idea that atheists think is absurdly obtuse and
monotheists think is absurdly obvious.

**Anorexic,** *adjective.* In a male, too skinny; in a
female fashion model, beautiful.

**Antagonist,** *noun.* The most intriguing character
in every story. Lucifer, for example. Judas, for another example.

**Anti-Christ,** p*roper noun.* He has already arrived
and is Chairman of the Board of a very large
transnational corporation, but we're not at liberty to
say which one. (See *Antagonist* and *Anti-Hero.*)

**Anti-Hero,** *noun.* A misunderstood hero.

**Apathy, Apathism,** *nouns.* From the Latin and
Greek *apathia,* meaning not caring about suffering.
A new, modern pseudo-religion has now come
forth, *Apethism,* comprised of those who claim
simply not to care about the question of whether or
not there is a God and an afterlife. Our Father

Below insists this is a pseudo-religion because it is based on a faulty premise and a dishonest tactical position: in reality, it is impossible for humans not to care about this question. After all, the recognition of a God or gods along with the caring practice of burying dead ancestors goes to the heart of what separates humans from all other animals, as witnessed by countless excavations all around the world. To claim that one simply doesn't care about this question amounts to claiming that one is indifferent to, and has not received any benefits from, the last hundred thousand years or so of human evolution—particularly those aspects of human evolution that separate man from beast. Humans are so constructed as to allow them to accept or deny God, but they are not so constructed as to allow them not to care about God. Frankly, *Apathism* is positively beastly—all puns intended. (See *Positivism.*)


**Apostolic, Apostolic Succession,** *adjective, noun.* From the Greek and Latin word for apostle, *aspostolos / apostolus* (one who is sent out). This is a very troublesome word and idea by which the Catholic Church has aggressively maintained for two thousand years that it is the one, universal (< L. *catholicus)* Church founded by Jesus and his Apostles, whom he "sent out" (*apostollein*) to bring his message to the world. These Apostles were selected by Jesus personally and were charged with the responsibility of creating a way to teach, convert, and serve the faithful; the Apostles did so all over the known world; and they then created a way  to pass on their responsibility upon their death to bishops (from the vernacular Greek and Latin *piskopos / biscopus*, meaning "overseer"). These bishops succeeded  the Apostles and they and their successors have continued oversight of the Church for 2,000 years. Unfortunately this argument may have history on its side, but fortunately for the last 500 years the troublesome concept of *Apostolic Succession* has been violently rejected by almost half of the world's Christians. So, we can still hope for the best.

**April,** *proper noun.*   As Old Possum noted: *April* is the cruelest month.

**Arabic,** *proper noun.*   The language God spoke upon becoming Muslim. Of course, no Christians could possibly speak *Arabic*, except for the fact that there are Christians who speak *Arabic*—and when they speak of the Christian God in *Arabic* they call him *Allah.* Well . . . that's confusing. (See *Allah.*)

**Aramaic,** *proper noun.*   The language God spoke when He became Jesus, even though there's credible evidence that God learned to speak only Hebrew, Greek, Latin, Arabic, and English, in that order. (See *Hebrew, Latin, Arabic, English.*)

**Armageddon,** *proper noun.* From the Hebrew *Har* (hill) + *Megiddo.* A small hilly area southeast of Nazareth where the start of The End of Times will take place—now a popular tourist destination.

**Art,** *noun.* Life imitates *Art* . . . and it's a good thing. Think of the alternative.

**Ashamed,** *adjective.* As some brother of ours said somewhere: If God created man, He should be *Ashamed* of Himself.

**Astrology,** *noun.* A pseudo-science that claims one's course in life is determined by the ordered movements of the stars and planets, when in reality one's course in life is determined, as all enlightened people now know, by random chance. Isn't it comforting to know the scientific, empirical truth?

**Atheist,** *noun.* A person who is naïve and egotistical enough to think that God doesn't exist simply because he thinks He doesn't exist. Napoleon was wrong when he said: A man cannot become an *Atheist* merely by wishing it.

**Atomic Bomb,** *noun.* A good start.

**Attention Deficit Disorder**, *proper noun.* What used to be called being a kid and is now called a mental disorder to be treated with psychotropic drugs.

**Aryan Race,** *proper noun.* A mythical people who were supposedly the first people to speak the mythical Indo-European language, an imaginary language, claimed *ex post facto* by the self-identified descendants of the co-called mythical Aryans, to have been the starting point of all the world's most important languages—that is to say, the European languages. Therefore, those who can self-proclaim their descent from the *Aryan Race* are, *ipso facto*, members of the living superior race. If this sounds rather tautological and self-serving, that's because it is.

**Authority,** *noun.* Something that must always be overthrown—unless it is the *Authority* of the senses. (See *Empiricism, Positivism.*)

**Back Office,** *noun.* A business term for the office in India that does the real work for a corporation's front office in the United States. The front office does no work other than collect the income and evade the taxes. (See *Out-Source.*)

**Bad,** *adjective.* Good.

**Bad Blood,** *noun.* Can always be improved with good breeding.

**Bad Conscience,** *noun.* Don't have one; opt for a bad reputation instead and never let your conscience stand in the way.

**Bad Language,** *noun.* Good diction.

**Bank,** *noun.* An institution that accepts deposits from you of your money and then charges you when you want access to your money; it also charges you when you are denied access to your money; it also charges you when you even think about having access to your money. What the *Bank* does with your money is use it for gambling (i.e. buying *derivatives*) and going on golf junkets.

**Bar Code,** *noun.* The mark of the beast. (See *The Book of Revelation.*)

**Bar Harbor, Maine,** *proper noun.* The extreme upper East Side of Manhattan. (See *Vermont.*)

**Base Instinct,** *noun.* The true bedrock upon which human values and ethics must be constructed.

**Beckett, Samuel,** *proper noun/name.* A great 20th century author who wrote in French and in English—who was born in Dublin but lived most of his life in Paris. His most famous work is his theological tragicomic play *Waiting for Godot*, which sums up very nicely the hopeless plight of post-modern man, who is forever waiting for some sign or word from a God who is unknown, unknowable, unkind, uninterested, unspeaking, untimely, and maybe unreal. Undoubtedly thinking wittily of this predicament, Beckett also wrote the immortal line, "When you're up to your neck in shit, the only thing to do is sing." So he sang, beautifully and soulfully—so sweet he could, and did, make the Devil weep.

**Beyond Good and Evil,** *book title.* The only way to live. (See *Nietzsche.*)

**The Big Bang,** *noun.* A 20$^{th}$ century theory of physics and cosmology that convincingly claims to prove the universe was created about 14.5 billion years ago; this has consequently brought a good number of previously reliable atheist scientists over to the cause of the Enemy. The Big Bang is a big pain.

**Big Oil,** *colloquial proper noun.* An oil cartel composed of a few companies based in the U. S. and Europe whose mission—achieved with total success over the last hundred years—has been the monopolized control of the world's oil exploration and refining capabilities. *Big Oil'*s motto is: Who put our oil underneath their sand?

**Big Pharma,** *colloquial proper noun.* A North American and European drug cartel for the manufacture and sale of legal pharmaceuticals; as opposed to (but related to) a South and Central American drug cartel for the manufacture and sale of illegal pharmaceuticals.

**Birth,** *noun.* The opening scene of a tragedy and it always involves screaming.

**Birth Control,** *noun.* The regulation of the number of one's children either through the deliberate control of conception, or the prevention of conception, or the prevention of the completion of gestation. During the 20$^{th}$ century there occurred further and improved methods of birth control in the form of voluntary and involuntary sterilization, technologically advanced abortion, and euthanasia, along with advancements in artificial insemination and genetic screening and/or genetic manipulation. The primary objective of *Birth Control* is to improve the quality of life of those choosing (or not choosing) to give birth to the next generation. In much of the First World, those choosing not to give birth to the next generation are on the winning side of the argument—and this has very intriguing implications for Our Cause. (See *Birth Rate* below.)


**Birth Rate,** *noun.* The proportion of the number of births at a given time and place to the total population, closely related to the *fertility rate,* which is the number of births a female gives over the course of her life (2.3 births per woman are needed on average to replace a given population) In the so-called Christian countries of the First World, the *Birth Rate* and *fertility rate* have been falling for about half a century. In most countries of Europe people are giving birth to far fewer babies than are needed to replace themselves. Inasmuch as God clearly directed His people to "be fruitful and multiply," He has good reason to be displeased with a lot of Europeans. On the other hand, Muslims (God's other children) are having plenty of babies— enough to grow their own countries and to add significantly through immigration to the populations of various countries in formerly Christian Europe.

**Bisexuality,** *noun.* The perfect storm. A human being just can't get into enough trouble being attracted only to one sex; so it is better to be attracted to both and thereby being able to get into twice as much trouble twice as much of the time.

**Bitch,** *noun & verb.* A colloquial term for a female dog or, in many American cities and general pop culture, a human female *or* male. From the Middle English *bicche* and the Icelandic *bikkja.*

**Bitch Goddess**, *proper noun.* In 20th century slang, a personification of worldly and material success, as in the expression, "He moved to New York to worship the *Bitch Goddess.*" In 21st century slang, a term for an extremely attractive female (or gay male), who is also too demanding and impossible, as in, "I'll tell you, that's one mean *Bitch Goddess.*" Well, political correctness be damned, the cold fact is as Our Father Below has said: Devilishly good slang captures certain truths and refuses to lie about them.

**Bitchin,** *adjective.* A contemporary term of strong approval and praise. We can't even guess how this happened, but it's *Bitchin* and we like it.

**Black,** *noun.* A color that, highly unfairly, often carries unfortunate associations of a threatening and negative nature.

**Black Art,** *noun.* Politically incorrect word for witchcraft, a part of the Wicca religion and now protected by clauses of non-discrimination in all enlightened societies.

**Black Friday,** *noun.* Any Friday on which unfortunate events occur that are contrary to the best intentions of The Enemy.

**Blackguard,** *noun.* 1) a low, unpleasant person; 2) a scoundrel; 3) a politician.

**Black Hat,** *noun.* The hat worn by the antagonists in old time Hollywood movies or nowadays by malevolent hackers chopping into the Internet.

**Black Hawk,** *proper noun.* A helicopter frequently used in offensive (or so-called defensive) U.S. military operations, named after a famous

Native American Indian chief who was trying desperately to defend himself and his people. (See *Indigenous People.*)


**Black Hole,** *noun.* 1) in physics, a point in space where the gravitational force is so immensely powerful that anything that comes near it is sucked in and destroyed; 2) in home economics, an object into which one sinks an inordinate amount of money, such as a sail boat, an old Mercedes, or a teenager, with no prospect of obtaining a return; 3) in national economics, a highly effective metaphor for the military and CIA budgets of the United States.


**Blackmail,** *noun.* A communication through which the speaker tactfully and helpfully suggest that an outcome highly unfortunate to the listener can be easily avoided by a timely payment of a modest and reasonable sum of money.


**Black Mass,** *proper noun.* Discriminatory, defamatory, and politically incorrect name for a solemn religious ceremony honoring Our Father Below.


**Black Mood**, *noun.* The alternate and better side of mania.

**Black Op,** *noun.* A term for a secret mission undertaken by the U.S. military and/or CIA, usually involving various forms of unconventional warfare, and conducted in such a way that its existence is deniable and that responsibility for it cannot be proven. (There *is* such a thing as a perfect crime.)

**Blackwater, Blackwater Worldwide** (new name, as of 2009: **Xe Services LLC**), *proper noun.* A private, mercenary, military company, based in North Carolina, which provides an excellent, invaluable service to the U. S. government in the form of trained paramilitary personnel performing offensive and defensive services, performed by private contractors (mercenaries) whose actions are governed neither by U. S. military rules of engagement nor by the rules of the Geneva Convention. Even Our Father Below couldn't think up a company this good. (See *Mercenary,* and *Xe.)*

**Black Race,** *noun.* A daring, exemplary use of hegemonic power by which the *White Race* delivered a devastatingly effective blow for hundreds of years against all the millions of peoples residing in and/or descended from the African continent. A textbook case of perfectly executed of linguistic hegemony. Our (black) hats are off in a ceremonious gesture of deepest respect.

**Black (** *fill in the blank* **),** *noun.*   As per all the various entries above, you get the idea.

**Blame,** *verb & noun.*   As most humans are far too proud, always be quick to *Blame* and slow to praise.

**Blasphemy,** *noun.*   Many great truths are deemed *Blasphemy* by many—the line between *Blasphemy* and brilliance is often exceedingly fine.

**Blessed Virgin Mary (BVM),** *proper noun.*   Well, most Protestants are not so sure she was blessed or virgin.   (What about that brother of Jesus named James who turns up in Matthew 13:35, Mark 6:3, and Galatians 1:18?   Where did he come from?   Or was he a cousin?)   Nevertheless, the *BVM* is a crucial figure among Catholics and an important figure among Muslims.   She is mentioned over twenty times in the Qur'an, but only a couple times in the Bible.   From Our Father's point of view she is way too popular and far too meddlesome.

**Blind,** *adjective.*   Love and Justice are *Blind*, and that's reason enough not to put one's trust in either one.

**Blowback,** *noun.*   A newly coined word used to refer to the unintended consequences of the C.I.A.'s surreptitious and illegal meddling in the affairs of other nations, particularly when these consequences are *Blown Back* into the United States and cause harm to the country and the people that the C.I.A. is supposedly sworn to protect. Well, every good turn deserves another.

**The Blues,** *colloquialism & musical term.* 1) The natural state of the human mind when allowed to be at a state of rest; 2) a form of American music that is descended from slave songs and created by southern blacks who were never allowed to be at a state of rest.

**The Book of Revelation** (aka **Apocalypse),** *proper noun.* The Biblical book about the End of Days, the coming Apocalypse, bringing about the end of the world as we know it. The only book in the Bible that gets things mostly right—and it's the last one of the lot.

**Born Again,** *adjective, religious term.* As if being born the first time isn't bad enough.

**Bourgeoisie,** *noun.* Out dated, politically incorrect term for the owners of the means of production, often to be found living in luxurious gated communities with fleets of doormen, some of them armed. (See *Proletariat.*)

**Brevity,** *noun.* Is the soul of wit but also the length of a politician's attention span.


**Bribe,** *noun and verb.* A holy offering, or to make a holy offering.


**The Brights,** *proper noun.* Without the slightest trace of humor, *The Brights* is the name of a 21<sup>st</sup> century atheist movement—which wishes fervently to avoid the word atheist—for those "who have a naturalistic world view free of supernatural and mystical elements." The choice of *The Brights* as the group's name is rather obviously intended to indicate that the members are indeed *bright* and in fact are *brighter* than those around them, those who might still be clinging stubbornly to antiquated, superstitious, and silly notions that there might be some sort of higher order above or infusing the World of Nature. Since we should all want to be natural and *bright,* this means that there should no longer be any place in our thinking—once we are truly *bright*—for such things as metaphysics, higher mathematics, astrophysics, theology, faith, divine law, notions of good and evil, etc. because they are not after all observable in the natural world. They are not part of the good old fashioned Natural Sciences and therefore should no longer merit anyone's attention. *The Brights* may indeed be as *bright* as they claim, but it seems they're not quite *bright* enough to understand irony—whether the intentional or the unintentional sort. For more information on *The Brights* and how to join the club, go to www.the-brights.net. And that's not a joke, that's a real web site. (See *Nature Worship.*)


**Broken Heart,** *noun.* Beware, for as brother Oscar said: How else but through a *Broken Heart* may Lord Christ enter in?


**Buddhism,** *proper noun.* An off-shoot of Hinduism, *Buddhism* is a religion that is based on thinking very hard about nothing. It has a devoted following in Tibet, some parts of Asia, and in Hollywood, California. It also has a substantial following in every college sophomore class in New England.


**By the Sword,** *Biblical expression.* He who lives *By the Sword*, dies *By the Sword*, which is vastly preferable to disease, dementia, and natural death. (See *Natural Death.*)

**Cain,** *proper noun/name.* The misunderstood brother. (See *Abel.*)

**Californicate,** *verb, slang.* To copulate in every possible position and then some. (See *Fornicate.*)

**Campus,** *noun.* A collection of academic buildings with the primary purpose of providing a controlled environment for young people to engage in recreational sex and drugs; and with a secondary purpose of providing a controlled environment for recreational education.

**Cannibals,** *noun.* Any and all indigenous people whom Christian explorers did not like and whose land they wanted to occupy. There are no *Cannibals* left in their native habitats, since they have all either been killed or been relocated to work on Wall Street.

**Capital Punishment,** *noun.*  A form of extreme punishment in the United States, especially in the state of Texas, which is applied almost exclusively to black males.

**Carnal Knowledge,** *noun.*  The kind of knowledge most sought after by college students.  (See *Campus.*)

**Cayman Islands,** *proper noun.*  The location of the most upstanding bankers servicing the most successful businessmen of the Americas with anonymity and annual returns tax free.  Switzerland with sand.  (See *Off Shore* and *Switzerland.*)

**Celebrity,** *noun.*  Some one who is famous for no good reason, or sometimes for two good reasons.

**Certainty,** *noun.*  Holding onto *Certainty* is like grasping hold of the wind.

**C.I.A.,** *abbreviation.*  The *Central Incendiary Agency*, the most important, influential, and incompetent arm of the United States government's Office of Foreign Affairs.

**C. S. Lewis,** *author.*  A brilliant and sometimes

devilish 20<sup>th</sup> century writer and professor too much committed to the cause of the Enemy.

**Camel,** *noun.* 1) A horse designed by an academic committee and not at all easy to get through the eye of a needle, but easier than getting a rich man into heaven; 2) A cigarette heavily marketed to teenagers through subliminally phallic imagery; 3) a camel toe is something else altogether and not the least bit phallic.

**Campaign Finance Reform,** *noun.* Like the Holy Grail or the Fountain of Youth, *Campaign Finance Reform* is a mythological quest for something long sought for but never found.

**The Canterbury Tales,** *proper noun.* A classic, narrative poem by Geoffrey Chaucer (c. 1340-1400) that recounts the stories, often humorous and ribald, exchanged among a group of English Catholic pilgrims making their way to Canterbury's cathedral. For proof of the wonderfully degenerate, disrespectful, and disheveled state of average Christian folk in the Middle Ages, one need look no further than Chaucer's devilishly funny *Canterbury Tales.*

**A Canterbury Tale,** *noun & British colloquial expression.* A long, convoluted story fabricated by a philandering husband upon arriving home to his wife in the wee hours of the morning.

**Capitalism**, *noun.* The perfect economic system to run the world. Designed most carefully by Our Father Below to take advantage of mankind's most basic instinct and character. (See *Communism.*)

**Capital Accumulation,** *economic term.* A new, politically correct and sanitized word for good, old fashioned, reliable, run-of-the-mill greed and profit mongering. (See *Doublespeak.*)

**Carbon Dioxide,** *noun.* A chemical that when generated by nature in truly massive quantities is healthy and vital, but when generated by humans in truly minuscule quantities is deadly and vicious.

**Care,** *verb.* As soon as one *Cares* for something it becomes one's enemy.

**Catechism,** *noun.* The book that defines the beliefs and rules of the the Enemy's Catholic Church; a significant alternative fuel source for the fires of Hell is provided by unread and discarded copies of the *Catechism of the Catholic Church.*

**Cathedral,** *noun.*    From the Greek and Latin *kathedra / cathedra,* meaning *chair.* The word *Cathedral* comes from the chair (or thrown) where a bishop sits.  Hence a *Cathedral* is a place for a bishop to sit around.

**Catholic,** *adjective.*    From the Greek and Latin *Katholikos / Catholicus,* meaning *universal.* Hence *Catholic* is an adjective meaning *broad* and *universal,* except when it is placed in front of the word *church,* because then it suddenly takes on the meaning of *narrow* and *annoying* to many people.

**Catholic Church, Catholicism,** *proper noun.*  The most troublesome of all religions, due to the fact that it stubbornly holds onto the dangerous and socially disruptive belief that there are certain unchangeable, eternal truths made manifest by Divine Revelation and by the ongoing presence of the Holy Spirit, working its way into the world— and that these truths provide a foundation upon which humanity can build its moral system.  The *Catholic Church* also claims, despite the protests of the Protestant Reformation to the contrary, that there is such a thing as the Universal Church that was founded by Jesus through his apostles and especially through Simon Peter, whom he personally designated to be "the rock" upon which his Church should be built.  *Catholicism* is so old fashioned and so quaintly cute as to be almost charming—if only it didn't continue to grow like a cancer all over the planet with over a billion adherents and counting. (See *Church.*)


**Celibacy,** *noun.* From the Latin *caelebs* meaning *unmarried, single.* The state of remaining unmarried, particularly for religious reasons, and, it is at least hoped, the state of refraining from sexual relations. *Celibacy* is required of priests in the Roman Catholic Church in the first sense of the word and, it is at least hoped, in the second sense of the word. The practical and at the same time holy idea is that by avoiding the hellish hassles of attending to the needs of a family the priest will have the energy to embrace the hellish hassles of attending to the needs of a parish.


**Chaos,** *noun.* The beautiful, blessed, original state of all things—and the blessed state to which all things, through entropy, are destined to return. Our Father Below rules. Case closed. (See *Second Law of Thermodynamics)*


**Charity,** *noun.* Should begin and stay at home.


**Chemical Weapons,** *noun.* When chemicals are purposely put into the air and kill people they are called *chemical weapons;* however, when chemicals are purposely put into food and kill people they are called food additives. (See *Natural* and *Organic.*)

**Childlessness,** *noun.* The pleasant, carefree condition of an ever growing percentage of people in First World countries, which tends to increase in direct proportion to increases in atheism, agnosticism, and apathism in said countries.

**Christian,** *noun, adjective.* A derogatory term first created by Roman Imperial authorities for the socioreligious movement that identified itself with Jesus Christ, from the Latin word *Christus* and the Latin suffix *-ianus*, a suffix that carried clear political connotations in that language. After about a hundred years Christians took ownership of the word and turned it into a badge of honor—a badge they still hide behind today. Happily, in many First World countries the word *Christian* is now returning to its original use as a derogatory term with political connotations.

**Christianity,** *noun.* The next to last (*depends on who's counting*) monotheistic religion; founded by Jesus and his Apostles in the 1st century of the Common Era after he realized that the Jews didn't get things exactly right. (See *Islam, Judaism*)

**The Church, The Universal Church,** *proper noun.* Let's be clear: The word church or churches refers to any church, that is, a building or a Protestant denomination. The expression *the Church* (with a

43

capital "C") refers to *the Universal Church*, which came before any church buildings and before any Protestant Reformation and *The Church* shall remain even after all the buildings and all the protestations are gone. Since the word "catholic" has always simply meant "universal", the Pope considers himself (along with his bishops and cardinals) to be in charge of Jesus Christ's *Universal Church* on earth, which is comprised of *all* believers in the teachings of Jesus of Nazareth. Most Christians remain in the "Roman communion" of *the Universal Church* and others have not remained within the Roman communion community, namely the Eastern Orthodox and all the various and sundry Protestant denominations. Despite the antiquity of so many of the Catholic Church's physical buildings—for example, St. Peter's and St. John Lateran, the church in Rome, where the Pope is actually the pastor. *The Church* (*the Universal Church*) exists apart from these buildings, above and beyond them, and above and beyond the priests, bishops, cardinals, and popes who are the imperfect and flawed earthly servants of *the Church*. Our Father Below finds this *church / Church* distinction highly annoying, but he is forced to admit that even he must grudgingly grant its logic and validity. (See *Catholic Church.*)

**Circus of Nero,** *proper noun.* A spectacular chariot race track built of white marble for the Emperor Nero on the Vatican Field in ancient Rome; it was later desecrated and cannibalized by the convert-emperor and opportunist Constantine the Great in order to build a church on the site in honor of Saint Peter—who had been (for good cause) crucified there, upside down, in the *Circus of Nero* as entertainment for the honorable citizens of Rome. It is a great tragedy that no trace of the ancient *Circus of Nero* has survived, except for a tall obelisk from Egypt that had been placed at its center; this obelisk now stands in the center of Saint Peter's Square in the Vatican, the sole remaining representation of the site's glorious, but forever lost, pagan past. (See *Saint Peter's)*

**Civil Union,** *noun, legal term.* A highly misleading term for an alternative form of marriage, which is an uncivil union 90% of the time.

**Classic, The Classics,** *adjective & noun.* As an adjective, *Classic* refers to the best, the highest rank. As a noun, *The Classics* refer the writings of the pre-Christian authors of ancient Greece and Rome, whose works sang the praises of war, paganism, eroticism, sophistry, and pederasty. It is most instructive, is it not, that the Christian West has and continues to bestow this paramount designation on authors such as Homer, Virgil, Plato, Aristotle, Sappho, Ovid, Catullus, et al. who represent a fine collection of—no offense intended—war mongers, sycophants, sophists, lesbians, and foul mouthed sex addicts.

**Cleanliness**, *noun.* Is next to Godliness, and He can have it. Have you ever spent much time with an obsessive compulsive during mud season in New England?

**Climate Change** (aka **Global Warming),** *noun.* The fundamental doctrine of the Environmental Universalist Church, established as Right Teaching (Magisterium) by the infallibility of ecological science. *Climate Change* is not the result of natural causes and is, by doctrinal definition, caused by human persons. Well, more accurately caused by Corporate Persons. Well, unless Mother Earth sets off a big mother (natural) volcano somewhere . . . then all bets are off.

**Cogito**, *verb, Latin.* Descartes's *"Cogito ergo sum"* (I think therefore I am) was a slip of the pen. It should have read, *"Cogito sum, ergo cogito cogito"* (I think I am, therefore I think I think). Hesitation and indecision are virtues of which Our Father Below greatly approves. They are the pathways to Deliverance.

**Collateral Damage,** *military term.* The politically correct term for Civilian Death Toll or for Terrorism. (See *Doublespeak.*)

**Comedy,** *noun.* That part of a drama or a life that comes before tragedy.

**Committee,** *noun.* A parliamentary, procedural device used to insure that as little can be done as possible, done as slowly as possible, and done with as many back room machinations as possible.

**Common Era (C.E.),** *proper noun.* The politically correct euphemism for the Latin abbreviation *A. D.* (for *Anno Domini,* meaning "in the year of Our Lord"), born out of Secular Humanists' charitable, if obsessive, compulsion to remove any and all spurious reference to God from all public discourse. Even though in this case it is not in the least bit "spurious" because the dating system employed still does, in point of fact, begin its count from the birth of Jesus Christ, establishing that year as the year zero. However, it's best not to mention that inconvenient truth in polite or learned society anymore. (See *Doublespeak.*)

**Common Good,** *proper noun.* This term used to refer to the welfare of the community as a whole, but in contemporary usage it has come to refer to the welfare of a corporation or a condominium association.

**Common Sense,** *noun.* The highly misleading idea held by otherwise sensible people that there are certain basic understandings universally held in common. Examples to the contrary abound everywhere one looks: It is *Common Sense* in Los Angeles to drive a car, whereas it is *Common Sense* in Manhattan not to. It is *Common Sense* in China to spit on the street because it is good for your health, whereas in France you only spit on the street when a foreigner speaks French. It is *Common Sense* in many Islamic countries that women should wear clothing to cover their heads, faces, and bodies in public, whereas in much of the Christian West women are encouraged to wear minimal clothing in public, revealing as much of their bodies as possible. It is *Common Sense* to come in out of the rain, whereas in arid countries people run out into the rain and dance and sing. It is *Common Sense* that a person is a human being, whereas under U.S. law a corporation is a person. It is *Common Sense* that if a corporation's stock price drops 50% the guys in charge do not get a bonus, whereas they get their bonus anyway. It is *Common Sense* that in the democratic United States people's votes decide who is elected President, whereas elections are actually decided by the Electoral College, the Supreme Court, and corporate money. It is *Common Sense* that you can rely on *Common Sense*, whereas . . . well, you can't.


**Communism,** *noun.* The perfect economic system to run the world. Designed most carefully by Our

Father Below to take advantage of mankind's natural instinct and character. (See *Capitalism.)*

**Comparative Religion,** *proper noun.* The name of a field of study developed in universities during the 20th century, the purpose of which is to compare various and sundry religions in various and sundry ways, in order to achieve the happy result that all religions are shown to be equal—and equally nonsensical in various and sundry ways. *Comparative Religion* is even better than atheism and even better than polytheism, even better than sliced bread—all blasphemous overtones intended.

**Compassion,** *noun.* A character flaw the strong cannot afford. (See *Compete, Competition, Competitive* below.)

**Compete, Competition, Competitive,** *verb, noun, adjective.* To strongly contend with another for acknowledgment, supremacy, profit, or survival. Thanks to the sacred texts of Adam Smith and Charles Darwin, we know that *Competition* is the essential, driving force of all biological, social, and economic life. The survival of the fittest rules from the petri dish to the stock exchange. The *Competitive* person is always superior to the cooperative person. He who hesitates is lost. Blessed are the strong of limb and gut, for they shall possess all the earth.

**Complementarity,** *noun.*    An out dated, cumbersome concept, expressed in Catholic theology, which holds that a husband and wife have a relationship of *Complementarity* whereby their two persons, via the *Complementarity* of male and female, compose a "wholeness" that is fundamental to humanity, to society, and to the procreation of the species. In a parallel way, there is a relationship of *Complementarity* also between the sacrament of Marriage and the sacrament of Holy Orders—these two forms of commitment composing two halves of a "wholeness" that is central to what it means to be human and to form binding relationships of commitment in the secular realm and in the sacred realm. Fortunately for all concerned, *Complementarity* is a complicated concept that most people no longer care to take the trouble to understand—and this is surely making the world a simpler, and we think better, place.

**Concern for Others,** *common phrase.*    As our brother Camus said:   To be happy one must not have *Concern for Others.*

**Concubinage,** *noun.*   From the Latin *concumbere,* meaning to lie together. Cohabitation of a man and woman without the annoying responsibilities of legal marriage and usually without the annoying responsibilities of producing children.   *Concubinage* is a convenient and superior way of life with an ancient history that is now growing steadily in popularity once again.

**Confession,** *noun.* An acknowledgment or disclosure of sin or sinfulness, especially to a priest, in order to obtain absolution. A nasty habit unique to the Catholic Church and the profession of psychotherapy—as if sin was ever in need of acknowledgment or absolution. On the other hand, in some circles there is now considerable argument as to whether or not sin exists at all. Our Father Below has made up his mind on that score, but his opinion doesn't seem to matter. (See *Sin.*)

**Confessional,** *noun.* A small enclosed place set aside in Catholic Churches where priests are allowed to take naps.

**Congregation for the Doctrine of the Faith,** *proper noun.* The body within the Catholic Church that oversees Catholic doctrine. It was created in 1542 by Pope Paul III with its original name, The Supreme Congregation of the Roman and Universal Inquisition. Yep, that's "inquisition" as in "Inquisition." It was renamed *Congregation for the Doctrine of the Faith* in 1965. Even though we've had our differences, and shall continue to have them, we've got to hand it to those guys—they make up their minds and they don't pussyfoot around.

**Consequentialism,** *noun, philosophic term.* A devilishly divine doctrine of modern philosophy first put forth by our sister G. E. M. Anscombe in 1958, which holds that actions in and of themselves are never good or bad or right or wrong, but rather that this is determined solely on the basis of the actions' *consequences.* Proper, good, and right actions, thus, should be aimed to maximize one's net balance of pleasure and/or to maximize one's satisfaction of specific preferences. Let's take, for example, the action of torture: An unenlightened individual (say, a Catholic) might hold the position that torture in and of itself is simply and always bad and wrong; however, if the *consequential* goal of the torture is to obtain information to capture and neutralize (kill) terrorists, then an enlightened individual would deem that action of torture to be good and right. You can see how sublimely simple it is. Simply plug in the action in question and then plug in the consequence desired—and, *voila,* the moral dilemma is gone. This is an example of one of those things that Our Father Below wishes he had thought of himself, but a college professor beat him to it. (See *Pragmatism* and *Relativism.*)

**Conservative Democrat,** *noun.* A politician who is a Moderate Republican in a state that is mostly Democrat. (See *Moderate Republican.*)

**Conspicuous Consumption,** *noun.* The socially acceptable and healthy display of one's growing purchasing power, the worthy goal of which is to establish one's superior social and spiritual standing above one's neighbors.

**Contempt,** *noun.* The greatest of all accomplishments. Do a man (or God) wrong and he can in time forgive you, but show a man (or God) *Contempt* and he will never forgive you.

**Cooperation,** *noun.* A cardinal sin that undermines competition and the natural law of the survival of the fittest; therefore it must be avoided at all costs. (See *Competition.*)

**Corporate Culture,** *noun.* A contradiction in terms.

**Corporate Image,** *noun.* Always to be reflected in a positive light.

**Corporate Income Tax,** *noun.* A complex phenomenon that may in theory exist, but is rarely observed in the real world.

**Corporate Man, (*Homo corporatus*), *noun.*** The highest, and probably the last, evolutionary state of mankind, which arrived on the scene in the mid to late 20$^{th}$ century, native to Fairfield County, Connecticut, but now hunting and gathering in many other areas; this species will, with any luck, eventually replace the entire *Homo sapiens* species.

**Corporate Personhood, *noun and legal term.*** An enlightened aspect of U. S. law whereby a corporation is deemed to be a "legal person." The best part is that a *Corporate Person* cannot be killed or be put in jail—and he can live forever, even if chopped up into pieces. Needless to say, this gives *Corporate Persons* several critical advantages over carbon-based persons. To err is human, but to forgive cheating, pillaging, burning, usury, and murder without personal liability—that takes *Corporate Personhood.* (See *Limited Liability.*)

**Corporate Responsibility, *noun.*** This is a devilishly disingenuous and distinguished phrase, coined to convince the inattentive and gullible that a corporation, which is a *Corporate Person*, can, like a real person, feel a sense of responsibility to society—whereas, in point of fact, a corporation's sole and only responsibility under the law is to generate profits for its shareholders, period. Profits for its shareholders, period. Profits for its shareholders, period.

**Corporation,** *noun.* The most ingenious business vehicle ever devised for those holding control of the means of production, and obtaining the most profit from it, to achieve their ends without having any liability or responsibility to society for the means employed or the impacts created in achieving those ends. (See *Externality.*)


**Cosmology,** *noun.* The second* most dangerous thing on earth, *Cosmology* is the study of the origin and the structure of the universe. The most dangerous thing about it, as all *cosmologists* now agree, is that evidence confirms the universe did, in fact, have a beginning—it hasn't always "just been here". And not only did it have a beginning, but it seems to have had a plan and to have known all along intelligent life was coming into it. It's way too close to that silly old story in The Book of Genesis, even down to the detail about "let there be light." It's ever so much easier to be an upstanding atheist if the good-for-nothing universe would just cooperate by being something that has always just been there, with no beginning and no ending. Because then it wouldn't give rise to, or even allow for, those damned troublesome questions of beginnings and endings! Time and time again, just when mankind has managed to get God out, He manages somehow to sneak back in by the back door. (*See *Higher Mathematics* and the *Anthropic Principle.*)

**Courtesy,** *noun.*  Public *Courtesy* is as a form of political witchcraft.

**Create,** *verb.*  As our brother G. B. Shaw said: God may have *Created* the world, but it's the Devil who keeps it going.

**Credit Card,** *noun.*  A *carte blanche* (pun intended) that allows the credit card company (i.e. a *corporate person*) to commit the crime of usury on the card holder (i.e. a *human person*) as many times and to whatever degree the credit card company desires.

**Credit Default Swap,** *proper noun, financial term.* Who in hell knows?  Well, actually . . . quite a few in hell know.

**Crucifix,** *noun.*  A religious, symbolic object of various sizes, consisting of a male figure representing Jesus crucified on a cross—used by Catholics to remind themselves that the founder of their religion was violently put to death by the state and through his suffering, death, and resurrection has offered salvation to all the human race.  The *Crucifix* may be as small as an item of personal jewelry or as large as a life size sculpture on public display.  However, no matter the size, the *Crucifix* is now considered by the enlightened courts of the

United States and the European Union to be a dangerous and divisive symbol, the public display of which is justifiably more and more curtailed with each passing year. Safety first!

**Crucifixion,** *noun.* The best method ever devised for the state to maintain control over the masses, by nailing malefactors to a cross on public display until their wonderfully slow and painful death. It was employed successfully for centuries by the Roman Empire with manifestly positive results. Unfortunately for the progress of civilization, the rise of Christianity put an end to *Crucifixion* with an edict issued by the infamous Christian-convert Emperor Constantine in the year 337. And things have been going downhill ever since.

**The Crusades,** *proper noun.* A series of military excursions into the Middle East by Christians during the Middle Ages for the ostensible purpose of taking back the Holy Land from the Muslims. After having stopped for several hundred years, with the dawn of the new millennium *The Crusades* have now taken center stage again in renewed force. (See *Holy Land.*)

# D

**Damn, Damnation,** *verb & noun.*　1) to bring condemnation upon, to ruin; 2) to doom to eternal punishment in hell.　In the current Secular Age, since hell has been condemned and shut down, *Damn* and *Damnation* have become simple expletives with no specific meaning.　As in, "Damn that dog, he's peed on the damned carpet for the last time!"　Clearly, dogs and carpets are not now, nor have they ever been, doomed to eternal punishment in hell.　That privilege was reserved for man alone.

**Damnatio Memoriae,** *proper noun.*　Ancient Latin legal term that referred to the practice of condemning and completely eradicating the name, public inscription, and all memory of a person, no matter how high in stature, who had fallen out of political favor.　"Condemned and removed from memory."　*Damnatio Memoriae* of individuals is no longer an official governmental policy in the Western World; however, the United States Supreme Court and the European Union Constitution are heartily engaged in a *Damnatio Memoriae* upon God himself—whose Judeo Christian name may no longer be used or recognized in any official document or building and, in more and more cases, is being removed.

**Dante,** *proper name.* A great Italian author of the late Middle Ages. He wrote a classic work known as *The Divine Comedy,* but it's not a very funny comedy; part one (*Hell*) is indeed excellent, but parts two and three (*Purgatory* and *Paradise*) leave much to be desired and consequently hardly anyone ever reads them.

**Dark, Darkness,** *adjective and noun.* The opposite of light. Because of rampant, unfair, and illegal discrimination, *Dark* has been given a bad name. But due to the rise of political correctness and inclusiveness, *Darkness* is beginning to regain the respect and understanding it has always deserved. After all, as the Psalm says: The *Darkness* and the light are both alike to the Lord.

**Dark Ages,** *proper noun.* A historic period, following the fall of the Roman Empire, when the entire population of Europe turned its back on all forms of paganism and looked toward Christianity for the peaceful ordering of society. With an uncanny ability to allow their Freudian slips to show shamelessly, professors later branded this period the *Dark Ages*—which might lead one to think that many professors tend to lean, shall we say, toward the dark side.

**Dark Energy, Dark Matter,** *proper nouns, terms in physics.* Well, for hard core Empiricists and Logical Positivists, there's a bunch of bad news here. *Dark Energy* and *Dark Matter* are forms of energy and matter that are <u>un</u>observable to current science, but the reality of their existence is demanded by indirect observations and relatively simple mathematical calculations. Since the late 20<sup>th</sup> century subatomic physics and astrophysics have demonstrated that vastly more is unknown (and possibly unknowable) than is known. It turns out that about 70% of the universe is made up of *Dark Energy* and another 25% is made up of *Dark Matter.* So . . . this means that what humans have observed to date with all their senses and scientific instruments amounts to, at most, less than 5% of the universe. No matter how many billions of light years out into the universe one looks with all those instruments, one is still observing less than 5% of what's there. So . . . Our Father Below begs to ask: How can so many so-called well educated people claim with so much vehemence that there are no such things as spirit or spirits, an afterlife, a Holy Spirit, a God, a Devil, Angels, a Divine Force, and/or forms of existence and forces different from the matter and energy currently observable? After all, at least 95% of what's out there remains beyond humanity's ability to see. As Edward De Vere, in the voice of Hamlet, said to his cousin Horace: "There are more things in heaven and earth, Horatio, than are dreamt of in your philosophy."

61

**Darwin, Charles,** *proper noun/name.* A great 19<sup>th</sup> century prophet and founder of a modern religion.

**Darwinism,** *noun.* The enlightened modern religion based upon the teachings of the Holy Prophet Charles Darwin (praise be to his name) which rightly claims that the true and only God is Natural Selection via Random Mutation. The following is chanted in university biology departments several times a day, while bowing toward the Prophet's birthplace: *"There is no God but Evolution, and Darwin is its prophet."*

**Deafening Silence,** *oxymoron.* The sound that comes after praying in an ungodly world.

**Death,** *proper noun.* The Blessed Prince of Eternal Peace and Darkness; Christians believe they can overcome *Death* and live forever in heavenly bliss. Well, they're half right—or rather, half of them are right.

**December 25,** *holiday.* The birthday of our beloved brother, the pagan god Mythras, founder of one of ancient Rome's most popular religions. Sadly, this date was strategically re-appropriated by supporters of The Enemy to celebrate the birthday of Jesus of Nazareth—this happened after the once noble Roman Empire had gone over to The Enemy's side. On a more positive note, however, during the 20<sup>th</sup> century this holiday became a major celebration of the excesses of marvelously materialistic Conspicuous Consumption. So we can't complain too much. All's well that ends well.


**Deceive,** *verb.* Remember, as brother Brant said: The world wants to be *Deceived.*


**Decline and Fall of the Roman Empire,** *book title.* A catchy title, but it didn't. The Roman Empire became the Byzantine Empire and then the Holy Roman Empire and then it metamorphosed into the Roman Catholic Church, which was forced to give up all its territorial possessions in the 19<sup>th</sup> century, but now finds itself with over a billion loyal subjects (and growing) all over the earth.
(See *Roman Alphabet, Romance Languages.*)


**Deconstruction,** *noun, literary term.* The *Deconstruction* of a house aims to result in its demolition—in a way that's pretty straight forward. Seemingly similar but different, in criticism the *Deconstruction* of a literary work aims to result in its demolition—in a way that's not the slightest bit straight forward.


**Defecate,** *verb.* To sh_t in Latin.

**Defense Contractor,** *noun.* A misnomer of epic proportions, a *Defense Contractor* is a corporation that makes *offensive* weapons of mass destruction to be used to prevent anyone else from making weapons of mass destruction, during a time of war, during a police action, during an attack on terrorists and/or insurgents, during peacetime, or during just about any time and for any reason anywhere that the powers that be may choose. (See *Defensive Weapon* and *Doublespeak.*)

**Defense Industry,** *noun.* Politically correct name for the Military Industrial Complex.

**Defensive Weapon,** *noun.* Orwellian Doublespeak for Offensive Weapon. When some one attacks with a weapon made by a *Defense Contractor*, that is taking Offensive Action. When some one hides in a house, a basement, or a pile of rubble, and sticks his head out to throw a rock, that is taking *Defensive* Action. Hey, *Offensive / Defensive*, this is not rocket science—well, in the case of *Defensive Weapons* actually it is rocket science. (See *Doublespeak.*)

**Degenerate, Degeneration,** *verb & noun.* To decline in physical, mental, or moral qualities; to deteriorate. The only action that comes completely naturally and universally to man as a creature of the flesh—so much so that even after he is dead and buried he continues to *Degenerate*. (See *Second Law of Thermodynamics.*)

**Degenerate State,** *noun.* The best state to live in.

**Deism,** *proper noun.* The belief that yes there is a God, somewhere, and yes that God did create the world we live in, but the problem is: he has absconded and left the whole mess just the way it is, or has degenerated into, and it seems therefore that humanity is now left to its own devices. Well, at least Satan hasn't flown the coop. He at least can be counted on. (See *Abscond, Deus Absconditus,* and *Theism.*)

**Delaware,** *proper noun.* A state that exists for the sole and only purpose of allowing corporations to register there and have as little oversight as possible.

**Democracy,** *noun.* A form of government that fools most of the people most of the time into thinking they have some say in their government some of the time.

**Democrat,** *proper noun.* A politician who protects the interests of human persons and corporate persons in that order, but running almost neck and neck. (See *Republican,* and *Corporate Personhood.*)

**Demon,** *noun.* From the Greek word *daimon.* A supernatural being that is a malevolent spirit; of course, now existing only in myth. The ancient Greeks were closer to the Ultimate Truth of Our Father Below's Vision: for them the original meaning of *diamon* was "higher self."

**Depleted Uranium,** *noun.* A radioactive substance that has been rendered completely safe by placing an adjective in front of it—except when it is used in the manufacture of ammunition, where it has the opposite effect. (See *Doublespeak.*)

**Depression, Major Depressive Disorder,** *psychological term.* This is the designation assigned by *The Diagnostic and Statistical Manual of Mental Disorders* for a mental disorder characterized by all all-encompassing low mood, low self-esteem, loss of interest in normally enjoyable activities, often accompanied by anxiety. *Depression,* anxiety, and other related disorders among teenagers in the U.S. have increased over 500% since 1940, and suicide has become the third leading cause of death for 12-24 year olds. These are impressive numbers, which demonstrate that the workers who are steadfastly committed to Our Father's Plan must be doing something right. (See *Psychotropic Drug.*)

**Derivatives,** *proper noun.* A financial term based on the verb "to derive." *Derivatives* are derived from two wonderful facts: 1) The Devil is in the details; and 2) An idle mind on Wall Street is the Devil's playground. This is a word for financial instruments (i.e. under-the-table contracts) used in gambling that are derived (as indirectly and obscurely as possible) from some real or, more often, some purely imaginary asset; and these trades (i.e. gambling bets) are always very heavily leveraged (i.e. they make use of a great deal of borrowing, as in 100 to 1, for example.). *Derivatives* allow, by their conscious and careful design, for the buying and selling of certain imaginary financial instruments, which instruments exist and operate entirely under the table and in the cracks between the rules that regulate financial markets. The primary objective of *Derivatives* is to generate huge, highly risky trades over the course of each year so that the most vicious high-roller trader-gamblers working on behalf of Our Father in brokerage houses, investment banks, and insurance companies can receive their well deserved, gigantic year-end bonuses—regardless of the benefit or harm of said trades for society at large. Capitalism is truly terrific, reminding us of the happy fact that the root of the word *terrific* is *terror*. (See *Investment Banker.*)


**Desperate Hours,** *noun.* Slang for closing time at a singles' bar.

**Detroit,** *proper noun.* Former capital of the formerly flourishing American automotive industry, now remembered primarily as the home of Motown records.

**Deus Absconditus,** *proper noun.* The Latin name for a God who made the world, saw what a mess it was, and then either hid himself so he couldn't be found or perhaps just absconded all together.

**Deus ex Machina,** *theatrical term.* Latin phrase meaning "God from a machine." This term refers to a theatrical device used in ancient Greek and Roman drama whereby a god arrived on stage (via a winch *machine*) at the end of a play in order to bring about justice and resolution. For a few thousand years now humans have been hoping for such a *Deus ex Machina* resolution to arrive on earth . . . and they are still waiting. (See *Samuel Beckett.*)

**de Vere, Edward,** *proper noun/name.* The devilishly talented and decadent playwright and poet who used the name *William Shake-Speare* as his pseudonym.

**Dice,** *noun.* The Enemy doesn't throw them—Einstein was right. But Our Father Below does.

**Differ,** *verb.* Never beg to *Differ*, just *Differ* diligently and devilishly.

**Diplomacy,** *noun.* The art of appearing to say Yes when actually saying No, and appearing to say No when actually saying Yes—all the while giving absolutely no one any reason to object.

**Discord,** *noun.* As Voltaire wrote in a letter to one of our friends: The world is a vast temple dedicated to *Discord.*

**Discretionary Income,** *noun, economic term.* A mythical concept for income that would go above and beyond the costs of food, shelter, clothing, taxes, transportation, education, health insurance, alimony, child support, and legal fees.

**Divine Revelation,** *proper noun, religious term.* An antiquated term for a certain method whereby Truth and a certain Ultimate Knowledge are passed down to mankind from a transcendent, godly level by the power of the so-called Holy Spirit operating through the minds, tongues, and pens of humans—a very unreliable, inconvenient, and dangerous way of obtaining ultimate truth. Fortunately for all concerned, no one in polite society or academia believes in *Divine Revelation* any longer, nor in ultimate truth, and most simply refuse to talk about the whole subject. (See *Empiricism, Positivism.*)

**Divorce,** *noun and verb.* The final stage of marriage.


**Doctor of Philosophy,** *proper noun.* Not the kind of doctor that does anybody any good.


**Dominatrix,** *noun.* A sexist, politically incorrect term for a female dominator.


**Dopamine,** *noun.* Chemical produced in the brain that is a neurotransmitter; it is associated with pleasurable activities such as sex and the affection known as love. *Dopamine* is directly involved in the brain's reward/punishment assessment and response; after the brain has received a particular stimulus repeatedly a condition can result that is known in neuropsychology as "reward prediction error," which for all intents and purposes is identical to the condition known as "being in love." Q. E. D. (See *Love*.)


**Doublespeak,** *proper noun.* A word invented by the novelist George Orwell in his classic, futuristic novel titled *1984* to refer to the carefully constructed, masterful manipulation of language by a corrupt and omnipotent central government in order to obfuscate and conceal the truth from the people being governed. (Don't worry, *Doublespeak* is just a fictional word in a work of fiction.)

**Doubt,** *noun & verb.*   Is the shifting mud under all religions' foundations.

**Downplay,** *verb.*   The verb that means *to ignore* in political discourse.

**Downsize,** *verb.*   Corporate *Doublespeak* for to fire or to lay off.

**Dramatic License,** *noun, literary term.*   Permission that the audience gives the playwright to be casual with the truth, allowing him to pretend—through *Dramatic License*—that life mimics art and is meaningful at the end.   The only playwrights who didn't make use of this license were some ancient Greeks and Samuel Beckett.

**Drink,** *verb.*   The Bible does have some good advice once in awhile:   Let us eat and *Drink*, for tomorrow we shall die. (*Isiah, 22:13*)

**Duplicity, Duplicitous,** *noun, adjective.*   From the Latin *duo* (two) + *plex* (fold).   Two are always better than one, therefore being *Duplicitous* is always better than being of one mind and straightforward.


**Dust,** *noun.* From *Dust* you have come and to *Dust* you will return. What comes after that is what's worth thinking about.

**E = MC squared,** *Einsteinian physics equation.* If Energy, $E$ (something non-material), equals Mass, $M$ (something material), times the Speed of Light, $C$, squared, then all philosophies based on pure empirical materialism might be in trouble. Similarly, modern physics has conclusively shown that mass and energy and time and space are interrelated in ways that blur the distinctions between them; therefore, a purely materialist analysis of the universe is bound to fail miserably. Most fortunately for the Cause of our Father Below, the vast majority of materialist philosophers, secular humanists, and college professors have yet to realize this, even though they've had a hundred years to catch on. (See *Quantum Mechanics.*)

**Easter,** *proper noun.* A holiday, originally of Christian origin, that in the United States has become a festivity celebrating the miracle of a rabbit laying eggs, involving a sacred consuming of candy, and a sacred obligation of buying and displaying expensive new clothes. This might be considered as a sacrilegious degeneration of something, except that any demonstration of due reverence for conspicuous consumption merits respect, appreciation, and encouragement.

**Ecology, Ecological Science,** *noun.* The science of determining exactly how much exploitation of the planet the human race can get away with and manage to survive in order to engage in still further exploitation.

**Ecumenical, Ecumenicalism,** *adjective, noun.* A feeble and vain attempt to stem the tide of Christian disunity which was so effectively set in motion five centuries ago by Brother Luther.

**Education Department,** *proper noun.* The only department at any college or university whose sole subject is teaching teaching and testing testing. That may sound like tautology. However, an understanding of the word "tautology" comes under the subject of English, which is not a subject covered in *Education Departments* and hence tautology does not concern those engaged in teaching teaching and testing testing.

**Egoism,** *noun.* The only known cure for the mental disorder of altruism.

**Egoist,** *noun.* A person who has his priorities straight.

**Election, Election Campaign,** *noun.* A mechanism of democracy in the United States whereby human persons used to be able to vote for the candidates of their choice, after hearing them personally state their positions and opinions on the matters at hand. However, since the U. S. Supreme Court decision of January, 2010, election campaigns have now been handed over lock, stock, and barrel to corporate persons, who will from now on determine the input and the outcome of every election campaign, since the Court has ruled that corporations may use as much money as they please to influence any election they please. (See *Corporate Personhood.*)


**Elective Surgery,** *noun.* Any surgery that a health insurer in the United States doesn't want to pay for.


**Embryo,** *noun.* The most controversial word in the English language—and several other languages as well. We're not going to try to define it. (See *Person.*)


**Empiricism,** *noun.* The philosophical doctrine that all knowledge is derived only from the authority of the senses, experience, and experiment. Period. And Our Father says, Right On! (See *Authority.*)

**End of Days,** *noun.* One hopes it's sooner than one thinks. (See *Book of Revelation.*)


**The Enemy,** *proper noun.* God, Allah, et al.


**Enemies,** *noun.* As our brother Antisthenes said: Pay attention to your *Enemies*, because they are the first to discover your mistakes.


**English,** *proper noun.* The language God speaks ever since He became an Evangelical Fundamentalist Christian. The only language spoken on the moon. (See *Aramaic, Hebrew, Latin.*)


**Enlightenment**, **Age of,** p*roper noun.* The *Age of Enlightenment* is a most interesting and ironic oxymoron, one which the contemporary Secular Age has yet to appreciate. *The Age of Enlightenment* was that age (c. 1600-1800) when faith in human reason and empirical truth replaced faith in divine reason and eternal truth; one small step for mankind, one huge step for Our Father Below.


**Entropy,** *noun, term in thermodynamics.* In any closed system, *Entropy* is the measure of the amount disorder, disorganization, and consequently a measure of the energy unavailable for work within a natural process. In a any closed system without outside input, *Entropy* always increases. In plain old English: Things left on their own run down and fall apart. However, here's the rub: in the 'enclosed system' known as the universe life has appeared and the presence of life decreases disorder and disorganization, while harnessing energy in countless ingenious ways. Life has transformed itself from very, very simple single cell forms to highly complex forms—and all along the way, over millions of years, always running counter to the force of *Entropy*. Despite Our Father Below's deep love and devotion to *Entropy,* there is something, some one, or some plan coming from somewhere or other that wants to, and does, run against *Entropy*— and we firmly believe that something is The Enemy.

**Environmentalism,** *noun.* A neo-pagan religion of the 20th century that is replacing many Christian denominations in the First World. *Environmentalism* is a matriarchal religion and the goddesses Natura (Nature) and Gaia (Earth) are its central deities who require massive human sacrifices, primarily in Third World countries.

**Envy,** *noun.* Is the spice of life.

**Equality,** *noun.* Balzac once said, *Equality* may be a right, but no power on earth can turn it into a fact.

**Eternal Truth,** *proper noun.* Like the Fountain of Youth, always wished for but never found, so all sensible people abandoned the search quite some time ago. (See *Enlightenment.*)

**Ethics,** *noun.* The system(s) of rules created by men (and we do mean men) to define acceptable conduct recognized in respect to a particular group, class, or culture. This is to say, all systems of *Ethics* are completely arbitrary and contingent upon which social group created them. (See *Relativism* and *Post-Modernism.*)

**Eugenics,** *noun.* An enlightened, early 20th century science (now making a comeback) of making humans ever more perfect by using any means possible to control, influence, and improve human breeding—including involuntary sterilization, selective breeding, genocide, abortion, euthanasia, and genetic manipulation. Just what The Doctor ordered for the new millennium. Onward and upward, scientific soldiers!

**Europe,** *proper noun.* The former seat of Christendom; no longer a significant force for The Enemy since almost no one there is having any babies; also, of the ever dwindling ones who are left, precious few go to church.

**Euro,** *proper noun.*    A new currency for all of Western Europe, the purpose of which is to make the Italians, Spanish, Portuguese, and Greeks pay more for everything simply because they are not German or Swiss.


**European Union,** *proper noun.*    An attempt to make the countries of Europe look and act like states in the United States.    Therefore, there is nothing very European or very unified about the *European Union.*


**Euthanasia,** *noun.*    Used to be called Mercy Killing and that sounded better; but honestly, we have to ask: How can anything that involves killing be all that bad?


**Evil,** *noun.*    1) a state of mind, or action, or affairs in and among humans that has understandably and totally excusably arisen from childhood psychological trauma or some other unfortunate events beyond human control; 2) a totally involuntary human response to random external stimulae outside of one's control; 3) a condition, or state, or force that humans once thought existed, but now realize can be explained by necessary and sufficient causes operating in the material universe.    What a terrible shame.

**Evil Empire,** *proper noun.* Any empire that is in competition with the speaker's.

**Evolution, Theory of,** *proper noun.* The manifestly correct theory that mankind is the direct descendant of beasts. Isn't that obvious? And that life forms change, without any direction toward any end, due merely to random mutation interacting with likewise random changes in the environment. *The Theory of Evolution* is the greatest single advancement for the True Cause of Our Father Below that has occurred over the last thousand years or so. Onward and upward—except (*oops!*) evolution has no direction and does *not* move upward. Onward . . . and sideways.

**Externality,** *noun, business term.* This is a term used in modern business practice to refer to any and all negative impacts that business activities may place onto society at large and/or onto the environment; the naming of these impacts as *Externalities* convinces gullible, inattentive, and/or corrupt members of the public and government that the corporation responsible bears no responsibility, since the impacts in question are *Externalities*, not impacts. (See *Doublespeak.*)

**Extraterrestrial Intelligence,** *proper noun.* Might as well look for it somewhere. Hope springs eternal.

**Exorcism, Rite of Exorcism,** *noun.* The act of expelling an evil spirit and/or malignant force from a person through the use of a religious formula and a spoken ritual. Since evil spirits have been thoroughly eradicated (like small pox) from the face of the earth, *Exorcisms* are no longer performed or necessary. *The Rite of Exorcism* technically still exists within the Roman Catholic Church, but—fortunately—most people think it is pretty much performed only in movies and in back rooms in backward neighborhoods or nations. See no evil, hear no evil, speak no evil.

**Eye,** *noun.* It has been said onto you: An *Eye* for an *Eye*, a tooth for tooth, hand for hand, foot for foot. (*Exodus, 21:24*) Let's just leave it at that and forget about the revision proposed by a certain Jesus of Nazareth. The first draft was better.

**Fabulous Invalid,** *proper noun.* The Broadway theater before the Disney Corporation came onto the stage.

**A Failed State,** *noun, political science term.* The final stage of any and all states. After all, time is on our side.

**Faith,** *noun.* The last refuge for the weak of heart, mind, and will.

**The Fall,** *proper noun.* Supposedly the worst time for mankind, supposedly the best time for Vermont.

**Fallen World (Fallen State),** *noun.* The one and only concept embedded in Judeo-Christian doctrine that is on the mark and 100% correct. Yes, the world in which humans are condemned to live is messed up, accident prone, and there is no way out but bodily death. What is there about the wonderful word *"fallen"* that you don't understand?

**Familiarity,** *noun.* Breeds contempt . . . and that's the beauty of it.

**Fashion Industry,** *noun.* The only business legally allowed to be based upon and to encourage starvation and slavery.

**Fashion Model,** *noun.* A very beautiful young woman with a very ugly eating disorder.

**Fast,** *adjective & verb.* As an adjective, *Fast* means moving with too much speed and consuming too much fuel; as a verb, *Fast* means slowing down and consuming no fuel at all—in order to have time to reflect and repair the damages done by moving too fast and consuming too much. English is indeed a devilish language.

**Felon,** *noun.* A person convicted in a court of law of doing what comes naturally. (See *Original Sin* and *Natural Law.*)

**Female,** *noun & adjective.* The gender that opposes the male gender—and has won. Due to a universal piece of human genetic programming, males are not as robust in embryo, womb, infancy, or old age. The number of male births in relation to female births is going down; females run every household on earth, excepting only the households of single men and male same-sex couples; there are currently more females applying, attending, and graduating college in the U.S. than males; and females in the First World on average live significantly longer than males. *Q. E. D.*

**Feminist,** *noun.* A woman who supports and asserts women's rights over and above men's privileges. (See *Women's Rights, Misogynist.*)

**Filibuster,** noun. Representative democracy at its finest hour, or several hours, or several days, or . . . several weeks.

***Filioque,*** *Latin noun.* One little word (meaning "*and also from the Son*") that by a miracle of acrimonious theology and grammar split medieval Christendom in two. A great moment in history for The Cause of Our Father Below.

**The Final Solution,** *proper noun.* Hitler and his gang had it all wrong; *The Final Solution* begins at Armageddon, as explained in detail in that most important and beautiful book in the Bible, *The Book of Revelation.* Even though Hitler was an altar boy, apparently he never paid attention. (See *Armageddon* and *Book of Revelation.*)

**Financial Advisor,** *noun.* Some one who professes to look out for your interests, but whose profession is to look out for his own interests.

**Flatter,** *verb.* To perform an action of insincere veneration—e. g., by humans toward old, worn-out gods and their representatives on earth.

**Flattery,** *noun.* Will get you everywhere.

**Flesh,** *noun.* The soft substance of an animal or a human body, as opposed to the bones, the brain, or the soul. By extension is the expression "the pleasures of the *Flesh*", which refers to all the higher aspirations of mankind. The 20$^{th}$ century's massive advancements in the art of advertising are based almost entirely on fulfilling the pleasures of the *Flesh*, largely through the titillating exposure of ever more and more *Flesh* of ever younger and younger females.

**Flirtation,** *noun.* This is the term for S*exual Harassment* when it is perpetrated by a member of the female gender—with the important difference, however, that *Flirtation* is not an actionable offense in a court of law. (See *Sexual Harassment.*)

**Flood,** *noun.*   The only reason God doesn't send a second *Flood* is that the first one didn't work.  Obviously the earth wasn't cleansed quite clean enough.


**A Fool's Errand,** *colloquial phrase.*   Life.


**Forgive,** *verb.*   To pretend to turn the other cheek in order to take revenge at a later, unexpected time.


**Foreign Language,** *noun.*   Any language other than English.


**Fornicate,** *verb.*   We used to know what this meant, but now we have no idea.


**Fossil Fuels,** *noun.*   Despite an unfortunate name, the more you get to know them the more you warm up to them.


**Fountain of Youth,** *proper noun.*   A magical spring whose powers could reverse the aging process, avidly searched for by the Spanish conquistador Ponce de Leon in Florida—now a health spa and plastic surgery office in Miami Beach.

**Fractal Geometry,** *proper noun.* A new perversion of nature that humanity has recently claimed to have discovered, whereby complex order and Intelligent Design can be found even in the midst of natural things that previously were thought to be the result of pure, beautiful, random chance operating in a wonderfully chaotic fashion. Is nothing sacred?

**The Federal Reserve System,** *proper noun.* The federal banking system in the U.S. that is under the control of a board of governors (*Federal Reserve Board)* and operates through a central bank (*Federal Reserve Bank*), so named in order to willfully mislead the American people into thinking that their country's government is solvent and has monies held *in reserve.* (See *Doublespeak.*)

**Fool,** *noun.* Even the Devil has something to be thankful for because it is indeed true that, thank The Enemy, *Fools* do rush in where angels fear to tread.

**Free,** *verb & adjective.* Brother Rousseau got it exactly backwards, the truth is: Man is born in chains, and everywhere he strives to be free. (See *Freedom.*)

**Free Love,** *noun.* There's nothing free about it.

**Free Lunch,** *noun.* Damn right, there's no such thing.

**Free Market**, *noun.* An oxymoron that means whatever one wants it to mean, as long as the rich get richer and the poor get poorer. Bravo!

**Free Press,** *noun.* When the United States was founded, it was deemed essential that the country should maintain a healthy environment for independent news reporting and newspapers, since an informed citizenry was thought to be the cornerstone of democracy. However, by the end of the 20th century it has now been realized that a *Free Press* is at best a superfluous luxury and at worst an impediment to the interests of the country's most important persons: Corporate Persons. For this reason, it has been deemed efficacious to place the *Free Press* in the hands of large corporations that can be counted on to look out for the interests of other large corporations.

**Free Speech**, *noun.* In American political campaigns *Free Speech* is not at all free but very, very expensive; while it may be exercised by human persons, it is exercised exponentially more by corporate persons since they can put more money where their mouth is.

**Free Will,** *noun.*   The Enemy's greatest mistake.

**Freedom,** *noun.*   Something that humans think they are entitled to and will do anything to get, and that is most useful for The Cause of Our Father Below.

**Fresh Water,** *noun.*   The substance on earth most essential for life.   Not yet traded on the Commodities Exchange, but this oversight will soon be rectified.

**Friend,** *noun.*   Brother Victor Hugo noted a beautiful thing: *Friend* is sometimes a word devoid of all meaning; enemy, never.   Remember, as Francis Bacon noted, it may be true that Jesus commanded you to forgive your enemies, but he never commanded you to forgive your *Friends*.

**F_ck,** *verb and noun.*   A colloquial word for having sexual intercourse or doing something bad to some one, as in "Don't f_ck me over, man."   The fact that these two seemingly different meanings have become linked together doesn't seem to bother people very much—a perfect example of not putting two and two together.

**F_ckin,** *adjective.*   An adjective that can mean *F_ckin* anything whatever the speaker wants it to *F_ckin* mean, and can be used in any location what-*F_ckin*-ever within any sentence.   The word no longer has any semantic association with sexual intercourse—clearly demonstrating that you can have too much of a good thing.

**Fundamentalist,** *noun.*   Some one who firmly believes that his religion (and it doesn't matter which religion) was best organized, best explained, and best structured many hundreds of years ago and that everybody since then has just messed it up—so the best way forward to step hundreds years backward.

**Future,** *noun.*   Never put your trust in the *Future*; it's so unreliable that it never arrives.

**Future Tense,** *noun.*   An understanding of the *Future Tense* of the verb is perhaps the only thing that separates man from beast—and precisely because he understands it, man can be more beastly than any beast.

**Gay,** *adjective.*   A word that used to mean happy, but now means homosexual.   Except that a *Gay* woman used to mean a prostitute, but now a *Gay* woman is a lesbian.   In contemporary teenage colloquial speech *Gay* means bad and/or unpleasant, as in "This lunch is so *Gay.*"   Is it any wonder people are confused?

**Gay, Lesbian, & Transgender Rights,** *noun & legal concept.*   Don't let the foot soldiers of The Enemy blame this one on Our Father Below—he hasn't had anything to do with it and, besides, he doesn't think anybody has any rights.

**Gang,** *noun.*   A corporation that has not yet registered with the Secretary of State.

**Gender,** *noun.*   A grammatical convention (found in many languages on earth) that classifies groups of nouns by their membership generally in one of two categories:  feminine or masculine.   Each noun is a member of one or the other *Gender.*   A similar meaning for the word *Gender* used to exist in reference to human beings, but this usage is insensitive and politically incorrect, so it will surely soon be completely abandoned.

**Gender Specific Behavior,** *noun.*   There is no longer any such thing, as per the above entry.   There may have been *Gender Specific Behavior* in the long-ago past, but that was an unfortunate mis-understanding which is now being corrected.

**Gentleman's Agreement,** *noun.*   A type of oral contract between well dressed males that's not worth the paper it's not printed on.

**Gigolo,** *noun.*   When a male willingly chooses to live off the earnings and gifts of a woman in return for companionship and sexual relations, he is condemned as a *Gigolo*; when a female willingly chooses to live off the earnings and gifts of a man in return for companionship and sexual relations, she is considered a wife or a mistress.   Equal rights be damned.

**Global North,** *proper noun.*   Where the big money is.

**Global South,** *proper noun.*   Where the cheap labor is.

**Global Warming,** *noun.* The politically incorrect term for *Climate Change,* or is it the other way around?

**Globalization,** *noun.* A late 20<sup>th</sup> century worldwide development that will, with careful planning and execution, faithfully fulfill Our Father's earthly mission.

**Gluttony,** *noun.* The sublime virtue of realizing that less is never more and that more is always better.

**God,** *proper noun.* See Allah. And that's the problem.

**God's Existence,** *the ultimate question.* Over two hundred years ago, Voltaire put it nicely: If *God* didn't *exist,* it would be necessary to invent him.

**Godless / Ungodly,** *adjective.* There is a subtle yet crucial distinction here, for example: a *Godless Age* is a time that has no God and denies a God exists; whereas an *Ungodly Age* is a time that doesn't deny that God exists, but instead refuses to acknowledge God exists and refuses to act as if God exists. The act of refusal is crucial. Our Father always prefers, with good reason, the *Ungodly* to the *Godless.*

**God's Image,** *noun.* Man flatters himself to believe he is made in God's image, when he is so often the spitting image of some one else.

**Golden Rule,** *proper noun.* Do onto others before they have a chance to do onto you—and always consult a lawyer first.

**Good,** *adjective.* Bad.

**The Good Book,** *religious expression.* Two words for this: Which one?

**Good Intentions,** *noun.* The road to hell is paved with them.

**Good Manners,** *noun.* The origin and purpose of *Good Manners* is to disguise bad breeding and bad intentions.

**Good Samaritan,** *proper noun.* Despite what the Bible implies, don't be one. The potential legal liabilities aren't worth it.

**Good Works,** *noun.* Are not the slightest bit necessary. You are justified by lack of faith alone.

**Goodness,** *noun.* It's all relative, don't waste too much time on this.

**Government,** *noun.* It's always bad; the less of it the better; better off just letting free will and the free market take care of everything. Amen.

**Grace,** *noun.* This is a term of high importance to Christians, with three key meanings: 1) the freely given and unmerited love which God gives and grants to humans; 2) the influence and spirit of God operating in a person to give that person strength; 3) a human virtue that has a divine (and unnatural) origin. Needless to say, *Grace* is a sore subject with the atheists, which is perhaps why they don't care if they remain in anyone's good *Graces*.

**Grammar,** *noun.* Unfortunately, as Nietzsche said, we fear man will never abandon his belief in God as long as he still believes in *Grammar*.

**The Greater Good,** *noun.* As if good wasn't bad enough.

**Greek Tragedy,** *proper noun.* This term has two, somewhat related, meanings: 1) a religious drama about pain, human flaws, and catharsis performed in ancient Greek theaters; and 2) a financial drama in the European Economic Community about pain, human flaws, and catharsis performed in contemporary Greek banks.

**Greenwashing,** *noun.* This is a newly coined word to refer to the practice, employed mostly by large corporations, of creating a public relations image which implies, or flat out lies, to create the impression that the business in question conducts its affairs in a manner that is ecologically responsible—and thereby, through a marvelous hypocrisy, said business gives the impression of holding firmly to the tenets of the new religion called Environmentalism. *(*See *Hypocrisy.)*

**Group Therapy,** *noun & psychological term.* Sessions in which tortured souls thrash things out together in this world; in the next one, *Group Therapy* is provided by Our Father in a stimulating environment with saunas, hot tubs, and peels.

**Half Truth,** *noun.* In the interest of economy and profit, never hand over the whole truth when a *Half Truth* will serve your purpose just as well—or better.

**Harm,** *noun.* A great man or woman should never refrain from doing *Harm*.

**In Harm's Way,** *colloquial expression.* Being *In Harm's Way* is a fact of life.

**Harvard Divinity School,** *proper noun.* A small, separate school located a half a mile away from Harvard Yard, where the study of religion is allowed under a loose affiliation with Harvard University. Harvard deems religion to be so dangerous and contagious that those who study it must be quarantined and kept a safe distance away from other students. *"Lux et veritas."* Oh, yeah.

**Hate,** *noun.* Pascal got it right: All men naturally *Hate* each other.

**Hate Crime,** *noun & legal term.* An unacceptable act of violence born out of a set of immoral convictions, as opposed to an acceptable act of violence born out of a set of moral convictions. Hence, for example: It is unacceptable to kill innocent Catholic Latinos because of guilt by association and that is called a *Hate Crime,* whereas it is acceptable to kill innocent Muslim Arabs because of guilt by association and that is called a War on Terror. However, be warned: this might be a subtle distinction on the proverbial slippery slope, so Our Father Below teaches that it is best simply to avoid convictions altogether. Violent crime and hate usually go together so let's just leave it at that—that's good enough for us.

**Heart,** *noun.* As the Talmud says: God wants the Heart. Well . . . so does Satan.

**Heart of Darkness,** *book title.* The title of an inspiring novel by Joseph Conrad, set in a wonderfully bucolic part of the Belgian Congo at the turn of the 20$^{th}$ century, filled with many authentic Indigenous People being lovingly cared for by a colorful collection of European ivory traders who further the charitable aspirations of the enlightened King of Belgium—a Gang of Virtue nobly carrying the White Man's Burden into the modern era. Highly recommended. Perhaps we're biased, but any novel that culminates with the line "The horror, the horror!" is well worth reading.

**Hebrew,** *proper noun.* The language God spoke before He became Catholic. (See *English* and *Latin.*)

**Hegemony,** *noun.* Another word for Imperialism, except sometimes—thanks be to Our Father— imperialistic power can be accomplished even without all those added hassles of expensive military occupations and troublesome colonial outposts. Brute economics, free trade, and cultural exports can fit the bill.

**Hell,** *noun.* A mythological place, like Hades was, no longer in use, condemned and demolished by modern, liberal, progressive churchmen and women. It doesn't exist, but if it did Ambrose Bierce—along with the majority of history's most interesting people—would be there.

**Hell's Kitchen,** *proper noun.* An affectionate name given to the best neighborhood in Manhattan, located on the West Side of midtown. [*Editor's note: Coincidentally, underneath the Hell's Kitchen neighborhood on a subway platform is where the original manuscript of this book was found, as noted in the Preface.*]

**Help,** *verb & noun.* As our good brother Aesop said (around 500 B.C.): "The gods *help* those who *help* themselves." The really devilishly delightful thing is that so many Christians think the saying comes from the Bible, and they think it goes like this: "God *helps* those who *help* themselves." Actually that version was said by the pagan playwright Aeschylus (also around 500 B. C.) and was picked up some 2,000 years later by the (almost pagan) Benjamin Franklin (who never said it was in the Bible). Now those of us who serve our Father Below may not be the best authorities on this, but we seem to recall that Jesus pretty much said a number of times and in a number of ways: "God *helps* those who *help* others." Isn't that exactly the *opposite* from saying "God *helps* those who *help* themselves"? Ah, ignorance is bliss—as well as a thing of beauty and a joy forever.

**Heretic,** *noun.* A professed believer who maintains religious opinions contrary to those accepted by his or her church—largely a Catholic problem. Among modern day Protestants there are precious few *heretics* because there are precious few opinions that can't find a home in some church or other somewhere or other. A few examples: Want to go to church where you can have several wives, some of them under age? Got one of those. Want to refuse medicine? Got one of those. Want to speak in tongues? Got one of those. Want you and your friends to make all the rules? Got one of those. Want to make more money? Got one of those.  Want to maintain the purity of the White Race?  Got one of those. Want the queen of England to be the head of your church?  Got one of those.  Want to maintain that every syllable, comma, and period of the King James Bible was written by God himself and is literally true?  Got one of those.  Want nothing to do with the Bible?  Got one of those.  Want to go to a drive-in church and sit in your car?  Got one of those.  Want to worship by watching TV?  Got one of those.  Want to meet single women?  Got one of those.  Want to rebuild the Temple in Jerusalem in order to bring about the End of Times?  Got one of those.  Want to meet once a week in order to sit together and have nobody say anything?  Got one of those.  Want to go back to worshiping trees and rocks?  Got one of those.  Want to dance in a trance?  Got one of those.  Want to sing in a trance?  Got one of those. Want to hold poisonous snakes up to your face and pray they don't bite?  Even got one of those.  For goodness sake, what's a *Heretic* to do?

**Herosexual,** *noun.*  A word newly coined and seriously being proposed as a non-gender-specific category for those who identify themselves as either gay or lesbian and think that the word "homosexual" is confusing. In as much as the suffix "*hero*" might be a tad overly dramatic and biased, we suggest that in order to even things out the word "heterosexual" should now be replaced by "*heroicsexual.*"

**Heroic Gesture,** *noun.* A waste of time.


**High-Minded,** *adjective.* A dangerous mental condition whereby the afflicted suffer from experiencing so-called exalted principles or noble feelings . . . and no good ever comes from that.


**Higher Education,** *noun.* An oxymoron of highly unclear meaning.


**Higher Life Form(s),** *noun.* This is a phrase that, by the end of the 20$^{th}$ century, has lost currency. It was (mistakenly) employed to refer to the general notion of there being life forms that were more complex than others, that possessed more advanced nervous systems, that engaged in simple or highly complex forms of communication, that even attained the level of self-consciousness; and this resulted in a hierarchy of life forms running from single cell organisms up to humans. However, contemporary evolutionary biologists have arrived at the counter-intuitive conclusion that all life forms are equally complex, equally well adapted to their environments, and equally necessary. Further, and even more significantly, no life form has a position of superiority over any other—such as, for example, the highly misguided and self-serving manner in which the Judeo-Christian tradition has assigned to mankind a position as the highest culmination of creation. Henceforth, amoebas and humans are equals. If anything, amoebas may be more deserving of admiration because they are not, after all, a parasitic life form that spreads like a virus, destroying more and more of Mother Earth's biosphere and annihilating more and more species in its hegemonic quest for domination. Our Father Below always said he never an amoeba he didn't like.

**Higher Mathematics,** *noun.* The most dangerous thing on earth—because it just might, in the final analysis, convince humans that a higher, unchanging, transcendent, and non-material order of some sort does exist and does underlie the universe in some fundamental and ongoing way. That's a frightening thought.

**History,** *noun.* A recounting of past events written (and rewritten) by the winners, on behalf of the winners, and for the winners.

**The Holy Land,** *proper noun.* You know you're bound to have a problem when you have three different monotheistic religions (and therefore three different shades of meanings for the word *Holy)* but you have only one place called *The Holy Land.*

**Hollywood,** *noun.*　Babylon, 2500 years later. Satan's Vatican City.

**Holocaust,** *noun.*　Don't think about it too much, besides it never happened—and even if it did (which we vehemently deny) it will never happen again (which we assure you). So relax.

**Honesty,** *noun.*　Is never the best policy.

**Honor,** *noun.*　The last refuge of a scoundrel.

**Hope,** *noun.*　Aristotle got it wrong: *Hope* is not a waking dream, it's a walking nightmare.

**House of Commons,** *proper noun.*　Living proof of the failure of common sense.

**House of Lords,** *proper noun.*　Living proof of life after death.

**House of Prostitution,** *noun.*　A house of the world's oldest profession. Also, either or both the House of Commons or the House of Lords—houses of the world's *second* oldest profession.

**The Human Condition,** *common phrase.* Dire straits, inside and out.

**Human Person,** *noun.* A featherless, biped, carbon based life form whose rights used to be protected by the United States constitution. However, over the last hundred years or so the Supreme Court in its infinite wisdom has consistently granted *Corporate Persons* more rights than *Human Persons* have, so it is safe to say that *Human Persons* will continue to be more and more superfluous and less and less important to the well being of the United States in the future. The wheels of justice grind slowly, but exceedingly fine.

**Human Rights,** *noun.* A misguided concept based on a flawed hypothesis: the insane idea that the mere condition of being human endows any sort of prerogatives in any way whatsoever. Absurd. The only *Right* humans have is the *Right* to fail, to fall, and to fight—a *Right* they use to the fullest. (See *Natural Law, Right to Bear Arms.)*

**Human Soul,** *noun.* Two of the most contested words in the English Language. Let us paraphrase brother Voltaire in this regard: If the *Human Soul* did not exist, it would be necessary to invent it. (See *God...exist.)*

**Humility,** *noun.* A waste of pride. (See *Pride.*)

**Hypocrisy,** *noun.* The *sine qua non* of all religion.

**Hypocrite,** *noun.* By all means, be a *Hypocrite,* just don't talk about it.

# I

**I,** *pronoun.* The most important word in the English language; the most important person in the universe. (See *Mine, You.*)

**Idealist,** *noun.* A seriously dangerous person who: 1) pursues high and noble principles; 2) is visionary and impractical; and 3) represents things as they should be rather than as they are. One has only to glance at history to see the incalculable amount of damage and hardship *Idealists* have caused to befall the human race.

**Idle Mind,** *noun.* A wonderful thing, a playground, in fact.

**Ietsism** (alternate spelling, **Jetsism**), *proper noun.* A brand new Dutch word that means "*Some-thingism*". This is a name for a range of beliefs held by people who think that "*There's something out there above and beyond,*" but they just don't know what and they just can't bring themselves to accept any existing belief system. As soon as our loyal European brothers have chased The Enemy out the front door, He somehow manages to slip in by the back door.

**Ignorance,** *noun.* Is bliss. Period.

**Immorality,** *noun.* The highest and best use of truly independent thinking.

**Immortality of the Soul,** *noun, common religious expression.* Ah, that is the question—that is *the* question.

**Imperialism,** *noun.* The natural and proper complete domination of a lesser country or countries by a single stronger country that has a limitless military budget and a limitless ability for making meaningless treaties and contracts. (See *Natural Law.*)

**Indifference,** *noun.* The best preventative medicine for just about everything.

**Indigenous People,** *noun.* People who used to live somewhere, but are no longer welcome anywhere.

**Indigenous People's Rights,** *proper noun.* Something Indigenous People used to have, but are no longer welcome to have.

**Indignation,** *noun.* Brings out the best in people.

**Individual Responsibility,** *noun.* An outdated concept which used to claim that since humans have free will they also have *Individual Responsibility* for their own actions. During the course of the 20<sup>th</sup> century, modern psychology scientifically explained that the main reason for parents is that through their inevitable and inexcusable failures in parenting they remove any and all *Individual Responsibility* from their offspring forever. (See *Original Sin.*)

**Individualism,** *noun.* The social theory that places individual liberty, actions, rights, and interests above collective interests or the common good. *Individualism* is always to be encouraged at all costs, as it is the crucial first step in establishing a valid and lasting compact with Our Father Below.

**Indulgences,** *noun.* The glorious wonders of the free market economy put to work inside the Roman Catholic Church leading up to the glorious and infamous Protestant Reformation.

111

**The Infernaltudes,** *proper noun.* This refers to a section of Our Father Bellow's sermon on the bank of the River Styx. There were eight infernal blessings delivered to the crowd and they are:

Blessed are the evil in spirit, for theirs is the kingdom below;

Blessed are the aggressors, for they shall possess the land;

Blessed are they who never mourn, for they shall need no comfort;

Blessed are they that cause injustice, for they shall have great rewards;

Blessed are the wrathful, for they shall obtain revenge;

Blessed are the evil hearted, for they shall see Our Father;

Blessed are the peacemakers, for they always fail;

Blessed are they that persecute the just, for theirs is the kingdom below.


**Infidel,** noun. Anyone who holds stubbornly onto any religion other than yours.


**Ingratitude,** *noun.* No good deed goes unpunished and that's as it should be.

**Intelligent Design,** *proper noun.* An ill conceived, controversial notion that there might be *Design* present in and underpinning the universe that would cause it to have just the right amount of hydrogen, carbon, nitrogen, oxygen, iron, sodium, etc. in it; that would also have in it a planet, or planets, just the right distance from a star, a planet having on it just the right amount of hydrogen, carbon, nitrogen, oxygen, etc. to provide an environment conducive to the appearance of life. And the further ill conceived notion that evolution of life forms on that planet would occur over millions of years, demonstrating an evolutionary process with direction from single cell organisms to highly complex life forms, which all employ a highly complex information storage and retrieval system, embedded in DNA on microscopic cellular and molecular levels, in such a manner as to result in the eventual appearance of intelligent life; which intelligent life would, after more millions of years, then evolve into intelligent life with consciousness and the ability to create abstract language as well as to conceive and communicate a notion of past, present, and future time; along with the most absurd notion of all: the discovery that there must be a Singular Creator Spirit (God/Logos) who set this series of events into motion and continues to guide their movements across time and space through physical laws that can be expressed and understood, to some limited degree, through higher mathematics and physics. Indeed, *Intelligent Design* is a tragically absurd and pernicious idea, exposure to which should never be allowed for children or young adults. (See *Logos*.)

**Inner Peace,** *noun.* A psychological state that is purported to be the objective of several out-dated religions around the world. For those living today in the First World, however, *Inner Peace* has been rendered unnecessary and unwelcome due to the cacophonous, incessant persuasion of sales pitches by the thousands delivered into human eyes and ears at every turn. The unfortunate fact is that those with *Inner Peace* make for poor consumers; consequently *Inner Peace* contributes nothing to the wellbeing of the economy or of society. In light of this, Our Father proffers some simple advice: *Give up, give in, give often, and give willingly.*

**Innocence of Youth,** *noun.* An antiquated expression no longer in current use since the *Innocence of Youth* no longer exists, having been sacrificed on the sacred altar of freedom *from* religion and freedom *for* free enterprise.

**Interest,** *noun, financial term.* Used to be called usury; now the politically correct term is *Interest.* Banks loan money to banks and make money through *Interest*; banks loan money to people and make money through usury.

**Internet,** *noun.* A marvelous invention for the world wide proliferation and encouragement of the virtues of Lust, Slothfulness, and Greed.

**Interrogation,** *noun.*   A word in *Doublespeak* that can mean *torture* whenever necessary; since torture is illegal, it is avoided by avoiding the use of the word.

**Inquisition,** *proper noun.*   An illustrious pogrom of the Roman Catholic Church during the late Middle Ages and Renaissance when some of Europe's most unfortunate and unwanted, along with some of Europe's best and brightest, were put to shameful excommunication or death at the stake because they would not abide by the Doctrines of the Church.   The extreme methods of the *Inquisition* were abandoned centuries ago by the Roman Catholic Church; however, these methods live on now in Promotion & Tenure Committees at all the best colleges and universities.

**Insanity, Insane,** *noun, adjective.*   He who thinks he can cure mankind's *Insanity* is the most *Insane* man of all.

**Insurance,** *noun.*   Legalized (barely) gambling.

**Insurance Lobby,** *noun.*   The primary source of income for members of the United States Congress.

**Intelligence,** *noun.* 1) the capacity for a sustained exercise of reason, thought, and understanding; 2) information gathered about an enemy or potential enemy. Interestingly, meaning number 1) is rarely present in meaning number 2).

**International Banking,** *noun.* All Hell broken loose all over the place.

**International Law,** *noun.* Whatever the most powerful countries decide to agree upon, for whatever length of time they agree to agree upon it.

**Investment Banker,** *noun.* Some one who makes money through actions (usury and variations thereof) that used to be considered in Christian theology to be contrary to nature. Dante, in his classic *The Inferno,* unfairly places usurers, and therefore *Investment Bankers* (along with plain old regular bankers) in the same circle of Hell as Sodomites—an unconscionable, unacceptable, and politically incorrect slur upon both. (See *Sodom* and *Derivatives.*)

**Irony,** *noun.* A rhetorical device that reflects a brutal fact of the human condition: that there is a certain glorious comedy in every tragedy.

**Isaac,** *proper noun/name.*   Son of Abraham and Sarah, who lived about 2000 B.C., through whom the Jews trace the ancestry of their religion. Almost sacrificed by his father Abraham, but saved by angelic intervention.  In the Judeo-Christian world, the heroic son.  (See *Ishmael* and *Anti-Hero.*)


**Ishmael,** *proper noun/name.*  Son of Abraham and Hagar, born about 2000 B. C., through whom Muslims trace the ancestry of their religion. Both he and Hagar were cast out of Abraham's family by Sarah.  In the Muslim world, the heroic son.  (See *Isaac* and *Anti-Hero.*)


**Islam,** *proper noun.*   The third and final (*depends on who's counting)* monotheistic religion; founded by Mohammad in the 7$^{th}$ century after he realized that the Jews and Christians didn't get things exactly right.  (See *Christianity.)*


**Island,** *noun.*   Every man is an *Island.*   Every woman an ocean.

**Jealousy,** *noun.* Foster and embrace it, as it goes hand in hand with love—and it also drives the world economy.

**Jesus of Nazareth,** *proper name.* The son (in a manner of speaking) of a carpenter named Joseph and his wife named Mary, who lived 2,000 years ago in the ancient area known as Judea and Palestine; Jewish; he was a bit of a prodigy in his Torah studies; he wandered in the dessert and spoke with Our Father Below; he became a teacher and a prophet as well as a revolutionary who threatened the domination of the great and noble Roman Empire. He claimed a special relationship with The Enemy, claiming to be the Son of the God and the Son of Man, whatever that may have meant. A small number believed him. Sensibly, the Romans, to preserve the peace, put him to death by crucifixion in Jerusalem, after a fair and equitable trial overseen by our loyal servant Pontius Pilate. Three days later some then claimed that this Jesus rose from the dead and left his tomb, which was next to a garbage dump just outside the city walls. This fantasy grew, more people said they saw this risen Christ (Messiah) in other places, and the mass hysteria led ultimately to the foundation of a new religion—a religion based on the teachings of this itinerant, penniless, and pitiful Jew, and founded on, of all things, boundless Love and Forgiveness. Of course, despite its short-term advances and purported assistances to humanity, we servants of Our Father Below steadfastly hope it is doomed to fail in the end.

**Jesuits (**aka **The Society of Jesus),** *proper noun.* The most learned and consequently the most troublesome religious order in the Catholic Church.

**Judaism,** *noun.* The first monotheistic religion (doesn't depend on who's counting*),* which gave Our Father Below a very bad name and took sides with The Enemy, making the controversial claim that He is the ONLY god. (See *Christianity* and *Islam.*)

**Justifiable Homicide,** *noun.* Is there any other kind?

**KKK,** *proper noun.* An old and venerated white supremacist organization that originated in the southern United States. Wish we had thought of it, but mankind beat us to it.

**Kill,** *verb.* Take care and remember the sensitive and sensible words of Oscar Wilde: Each man *Kills* the thing he loves.

**Kind,** *adjective.* Be *Kind* to animals. Period.

**Kindness,** *noun.* To be avoided, except: "a cruel *Kindness*" being one exception, and "to kill with *Kindness*" being the other.

**Kingdom of Christ,** *religious term.* As a man named Montesquieu said: No kingdom has had as many civil wars as the *Kingdom of Christ*.

**Know Thyself,** *philosophic expression.* An inconvenient and inadvisable command handed down from the ancient Greeks—largely ignored.


**Knowledge,** *noun.* Brother Socrates had it backwards. He should have said: There is only one good, Ignorance; and one evil, *Knowledge.* This is clearly explained in the Book of Genesis, specifically the part about Adam and Eve eating the fruit from the Tree of *Knowledge*—and it's all been delightfully downhill ever since.

**Last Will and Testament,** *legal term.* Your last, best hope of getting back at people you don't like.

**Latin,** *proper noun.* The language God spoke when He became Catholic. A dead language now, except in the Vatican—try not to think about the subtext. (See *Arabic, English, and Hebrew.*)

**Law School,** *noun.* A specialized training school that instructs naïve and impressionable students in how to use state and federal laws to protect the interests of corporations.

**The Law of Unintended Consequences,** *newly minted phrase.* This is a law that states: If you let the C.I.A. (or some other Gang of Virtue) throw sh_t at a fan, sooner or later the sh_t is going to hit the fan and there will be plenty of *Unintended Consequences*—and unintended victims. (See *Blowback.*)

**Left,** *adjective and proper noun.* The one that doesn't know what the right one is doing—in politics as in life. (See *Right.*)

**Lent,** *proper noun, religious term.* An annual period of religious fasting and penance, which was established in order to provide a reason for Mardi Gras.

**The Lesser of Two Evils,** *colloquial expression.* Never settle for that.

**Liberal**, *noun and adjective.* A term of severe reprobation used by Republican politicians for anyone they don't like who went to college or finished high school. (See *Liberal Arts.*)

**Liberal Arts,** *proper noun.* From the ancient Latin *Artes Liberales*, meaning *arts and learning befitting a free person,* as opposed to a slave—keeping in mind that in those good old days almost half the population of Rome were slaves. In the Classical Age, the *Liberal Arts* were those subjects necessary to make the free youths of Greece and Rome into well informed citizens. In the present age, the *Liberal Arts* appear to Conservatives to be those subjects necessary to make free thinking youths of America into misinformed Liberals. (See *Liberal.*)

**Liberation Theology,** *noun.* Come on, as if any theology could ever be liberating. Nonetheless, *Liberation Theology* was a misguided movement within the 20<sup>th</sup> century Catholic Church which claimed that it was the sacred duty of the Church to comfort the afflicted and afflict the comfortable, thereby to obtain social justice for the world's poor and downtrodden. Fortunately for the fortunate, the Vatican decided this was a bridge too far and ordered a strategic retreat.

**Lie,** *verb.* To speak the truth in political discourse.

**Life,** *noun.* Yes, *Life* is short . . . but its misery makes it seem long.

**Life, Liberty, and the Pursuit of Happiness,** *well known phrase.* Some people think they are endowed with these as inalienable rights. What a positively ridiculous idea. (See *Positivism*.)

**Limbo,** *proper noun.* A theological term for the abode after death of unbaptized infants and the pagan righteous who died before the coming of Christ. It became filled to capacity and had to be officially shut down in the 20<sup>th</sup> century.

125

**Limited Liability,** *noun and legal term.* The cornerstone of enlightened American corporate law, *Limited Liability* affords almost bullet-proof legal protection to those who run corporations, absolving them from legal and/or financial liability for actions performed by the corporations that they are running. The noble purpose of *Limited Liability* is to encourage amoral, or perhaps immoral, behavior that will result in better and better corporate profits. As brother Machiavelli said so succinctly: The ends justify the means. (See *Amoral, Immoral.)*

**Listen,** *verb.* To give attention with one's ears and mind to something or some one; to attend closely to what some one else is saying. Usually a waste of time.

**Literary Critic,** *noun.* A bulldozer, except without as much empathy.

**Lobbyist,** *noun.* A political appointee or politician between jobs.

**Logos,** *proper noun.* 1) This is a controversial philosophical and theological term for the rational principle that governs and develops the universe, hardcore evolutionists' claims to the contrary not-withstanding. 2) In Christian theology (*see Gospel* *of John 1:1)* this *Logos* is one with God the Father, the Holy Spirit, and Jesus, who is the *Logos* made flesh, "The Word made flesh." *Logos* is the ancient Greek word for speech, word, thought, discourse, proportion; *Logos* is the root of the words *logic* and *logical.* Interestingly, modern secular humanists, who are the first to reject all of Christian theology, are also the first to claim that they are, above all else and above everyone else, *logical*—in blissful ignorance of the theological underpinnings of the concept of *logic* itself. This is to say: Unless the universe is informed by the *Logos,* by some overarching and interwoven *logic,* then what on earth would be the point of humans developing *logical* analysis? What end would it serve? *Logical* analysis would have no purpose or meaning unless the universe itself in some deep way manifests *logical* processes, which can be understood through *logical* thought. If the universe is nothing but random events governed by random chance, full of sound and fury signifying nothing, then why even bother with any attempt to understand it? The entire endeavor of science would be hopeless and would mean nothing at all unless there is a *logical order (Logos)* present in the world to be scientifically discovered and explained. Well, *fortunately for Our Cause,* by the late 20th century this simple realization has been largely forgotten.


**Logical Positivism,** *proper noun.* A school of philosophy based on a contradiction in terms. (See *Logos* and *Positivism.*)

127

**Lolita,** *proper noun, name.* A girl's given name, made famous by the novelist Vladimir Nabokov in his novel of the same name, which follows the sensual exploits of epic proportions of an under-age, over-sexed girl named *Lolita*. The book provides an inspiring role model for young girls and it should officially be required reading in all junior high schools of the Western World—unofficially, it already is in many locations. The fashion and advertising industries seem to have made *Lolita* required reading for quite some time now.

**Los Angeles,** *proper noun.* Despite its name, very few angels are found there.

**Love,** *verb and noun.* A misdirected affection always misguided in this misanthropic world. As in, "I love you," or "Love thy neighbor," or "God is love." *Amo, amas, amat . . .* not.

**Love of Truth,** *noun, colloquial phrase.* Of all the *Loves* one can experience, the *Love of Truth* is the worst and most dangerous.

**Lyric Poetry,** *noun.* A form of writing based on the strange idea that there might be something worth caring deeply about and, stranger still, that there might be something worth saying about it.

**Lucifer,** *proper noun/name.*   The name of the best and brightest, but most proud and rebellious, archangel who had a falling out with God (i.e. The Enemy) and was ejected from the heavenly realm to form his own realm known affectionately as Hell. Also known to Judeo-Christians as the Devil or Satan. If *Lucifer* is really so bad, then why on earth does his name mean "Light Bringer", from the Latin *lux* (light) + *fer* (to   bring)? How can an antagonist with a name that good be all that bad?   (See *Satan.*)


**Lying,** *noun (gerund).*   *Lying* is often the only right thing to do. And this is not a lie.

# M

**Madonna,** *proper noun/name.* A late 20<sup>th</sup> century pop singer. Any other meaning of the English word *Madonna* has fallen out of use.

**Madonna and Child,** *proper noun/name.* A late 20<sup>th</sup> century pop singer in a photo op with her adopted baby.

**Machiavelli, Nicolo,** *proper noun/name.* Great Renaissance Italian statesman, philosopher, and brother who ushered in modern political theory, finally freeing political and military decisions of European rulers (and their descendants today) from recourse to any supposedly higher values that purport to originate from a sacred realm—such as, for example, the values taught by Jesus of Nazareth. *Machiavelli* stated a beautiful, eternal truth very simply: "The ends justify the means." A ruler's end is to win and maintain the upper position, so those who rule have a duty to use any and all means to achieve that end. Our Father couldn't have said it better himself. (See *Unconventional Warfare.*)

**Machismo,** *noun.* 1) a sexist, politically incorrect display of maleness by a male; 2) the male version of femininity, except that *Machismo* is now disallowed in all enlightened societies. (See *Neuterismo.*)


**Majority Rule,** *noun, term in political science.* The Achilles heel of democracy.


**Mal-,** a prefix almost always meaning "good."


**Male,** *noun & adjective.* The gender that starts all the wars and wins all the wars; therefore is the superior one.


**Malice, Malicious,** *noun, adjective.* The wonderful thing is: *Malicious* men have to die, but their *Malice* can live on after them.


**Malthus, Thomas Robert,** *proper noun/name.* Late 18th century English economist and clergyman who was steadfastly convinced of the pleasant idea that human populations will always grow faster than they can feed themselves, which will inevitably lead to most of the world's populations regularly starving to death on massive scales. Unfortunately for all concerned, his theory was only wishful thinking. He was 100% wrong. Some two hundred years after his dire prediction a growing percentage of the world's population is becoming obese. This is a pity because it would have made things so much easier if *Malthus* had been right.


**Mammon,** *proper noun.* The Supreme God of the world's most powerful religion. His chief temples are in New York, London, and Tokyo.


**Man,** *noun.* 1) a being composed of matter and spirit, lost somewhere between heaven and hell, both being places he no longer believes in; 2) a sexist, politically incorrect term for "person" or "human being" or "humanity".


**Manifest Destiny,** *proper noun.* When a country decides what it really, really wants to do then the accomplishment of that goal is called *Manifest Destiny*—and, as an added benefit, the really handy thing is that *Manifest Destiny* justifies any and all means employed to accomplish that goal. After all, you can't fight fate. (See *Machiavelli.*)


**Manipulate,** *verb.* To persuade with great subtlety and creativity.


**Manufactured Consent,** *noun.* When the people's agreement to policy is orchestrated by The Powers

That Be in a socialist state, it is propaganda. When the people's agreement to policy is orchestrated by The Powers That Be in a capitalist state, it is *Manufactured Consent*—carried out by corporate interests that control commercial mass media, operating via massive influence peddling accomplished via paid lobbyists, paid air time, and paid politicians. When the people's agreement to policy can no longer be orchestrated by The Powers That Be in any way, shape, or form, then the time is usually ripe for a coup or a revolution. (See *Revolution.*)

**Market Self-Regulation,** *noun, financial term.* This is a wonderfully demonic idea, with the pun on the word "demon" (<Greek *daimon,* guiding spirit) intended. A group of late 20$^{th}$ century financiers and economists came up with the idea that stock and bond markets as well as currency and commodity exchanges and all financial markets of whatever sort would somehow in some miraculous way *Self-Regulate* merely by allowing the forces of free market capitalism to operate and run their course—perhaps (may we be so bold as to suggest) because these markets were thought to have some unseen demon inside them making split second, serendipitous decisions for the welfare of the trader-gamblers and humanity as a whole. Well, by the end of the first decade of the new millennium there was a mountain of evidence (and bad debt) proving that *Market Self-Regulation* is a kettle of delightfully stinking fish. While we sincerely admire

the devastating results achieved, we must in all honesty point out that even good old Adam Smith knew better when he wrote *The Wealth of Nations* over 200 years ago. (Psst, does anyone on Wall Street know how to read?) *Market Self-Regulation* . . . who thinks this stuff up? Do they get PhD's to think this stuff up? Absolutely brilliant! Congratulations! Couldn't have done better ourselves.

**Marketplace,** *noun.* The best place to let all problems be solved—at least according to the wisdom of neo-liberal, free market economists.

**Marriage,** noun. A legally binding (but not too binding) contractual relationship between any two or more people of any sex or age that is sanctioned by the state and/or by whatever church can be found to do it—entered into because of certain tax and health insurance advantages. Blessed be the tie that binds . . . loosely.

**Marx, Karl,** *proper noun/name.* The great 19th century philosopher whose works inspired millions of men to build The People's heaven-on-earth and thereby paved the way for creating hell-on-earth for people. (See *Communism* and *Revolution*.)

**Masochist,** *noun.* Any person who willingly makes the choice to go on living day after miserable day.

**Mass,** *proper noun.*   Catholic term for the congregation's gathering in celebration of the Eucharist, the Roman Catholic religious service led by a priest. Most interesting to note is the fact that the origin of the term's colloquial use among the laity may well stem from the original Latin words spoken at the final moment of the service: *"Ite, Missa est" ("You may go, the Mass is finished")*— indicating just how very much the congregation just wanted to get out of there. Well, out of the frying pan and into the fire, as they say.

**Mass Communication,** *noun.*   A contradiction in terms.

**Master Race,** *proper noun.*   The race that corresponds to the race of the speaker.

**Materialism,** *noun.*   1) The One True Religion, which holds that nothing exists except physical, material reality and that true knowledge is obtained only from empirical analysis; 2) by analogy, an alternative meaning in common usage is the belief that the primary goal of the Good Life is to purchase, own, and enjoy more and more pos- sessions.  Since the late 20$^{th}$ century, meanings 1) and 2) have come to rule the roost of the First World's hen house.

**Matriarchy,** *noun.* A superior and increasingly dominant form of social organization whereby the mother is the supreme authority in the family, and descent is reckoned through the female line, with or without a father being present, most frequently without a father being present. (See *Patriarchy.*)

**Mercy,** *noun.* A dangerous waste of sentiment.

**Merciful,** *adjective.* Our Father Above is said to be *Merciful*, Our Father Below is not.

**Medical Insurance (Health Care),** *noun.* In the U. S. they have two words for that: Ha! and No!

**The Meek,** *collective noun.* *The Meek* shall inherit the earth—after it has been used up and discarded by the powerful and the rich. And that's as it should be.

**Mendacious,** *adjective.* A positive character trait that is evident by a polite attempt to cloak the truth in only the most positive terms. As in "The interest rate on this credit card is 5%," or "The collateral damage was within acceptable parameters."

**Mercenary,** *noun.* A professional combat soldier willing to kill others not for a philosophical cause but for an honest living.

**Mercy,** *noun.* Pray for it, it can't hurt. If you don't, it can hurt. But nobody listens.

**Meritocracy,** *noun.* A mythical system whereby individuals are rewarded based solely on the merit of their qualifications. For example, the admissions process at Yale.

**Metaphysics,** *noun.* From the ancient Greek *meta* (beyond) + *physika* (natural things). This is an outmoded term, no longer in use, for a branch of philosophy that used to be concerned with that which was thought to be *beyond physics*, beyond the physical, and having to do with first principles, cosmology, and ontology. Since empirical science has demonstrated to all sensible, well educated people that physical causes are both necessary and sufficient to explain absolutely everything in the universe, *Metaphysics* is no longer necessary or worthwhile.

**Miami,** *proper noun.* The capital of South America.

**Miami Beach,** *proper noun.* The southernmost borough of New York City.

**Migrant Labor,** *noun.* The politically correct term for a modern form a slavery, except with *Migrant Labor* the overhead costs for maintaining the work force are, happily, far lower than was the case under the slave system.

**Militia Movement,** *noun.* Terrorists for White, Anglo-Saxon, Protestant supremacist religions.

**Military Industrial Complex,** *noun.* A match made in heaven . . . or maybe someplace else. A politically incorrect name for the *Defense Industry.*

**Military Intelligence,** *noun.* An oxymoron justifying deadly force.

**Mine,** *possessive pronoun.* The second most important word in the English language. (See the pronoun "*I*")

**Misanthrope,** *noun.* From the ancient Greek *misos* (hate) + *anthropos* (humanity). 1) some one who hates human kind; 2) a wise man.

**Miscommunication,** *noun.* The best and most useful form of communication.

**Misinform,** *verb.* To inform in a press release.

**Misogynist,** *noun.* The male version of a feminist, except he is attempting to assert rights that he no longer has. (See *Feminist.*)

**Missionary,** *noun.* A Christian willing to go into the midst of non-Christian, economically disadvantaged people to make them ready to become even more economically disadvantaged upon the arrival of other Christians soon to follow.

**Missionary Position,** *noun.* The only bodily position for sexual intercourse that meets with Our Father Below's disapproval.

**Mistress,** *noun.* A sexist, politically incorrect term for an adulteress—oops, we meant to say female adulterer. (See *Gigolo.*)

**Moderate Republican,** *noun.* A politician who is a Conservative Democrat in a state that is Republican. (See *Conservative Democrat.*)

**Modesty,** *noun.* In the world formerly known as western Christendom *Modesty* is no longer required of anyone; in the Islamic world *Modesty* is still required of everyone. In all modesty, we must be so bold as to suggest there's a problem here. (See *Common Sense.*)

**A Moment of Silent Prayer,** *colloquial expression.* Inappropriate, coercive, and divisive behavior to be scrupulously avoided in polite society or public school.

**Monotheism,** *noun.* The religious belief that there is only one Supreme God, rather than many gods, and that all the universe is this God's creation. Over 50% of humans on earth have fallen victim to this perverse yet alluring idea—and both Christianity and Islam, we are sorry to report, are continuing to grow with each passing year.

**A Moral Dilemma,** *noun.* Being forced to decide between the lesser or the greater of two evils.

**A Moral Hazard,** *technical legal and business term.* An unfair and inappropriate term for a situation, process, or system that creates an environment likely to engender selfish and/or illegal behavior likely to harm others or others' business interests. For example: buying fire insurance on one's property for more than it is worth; or having a 5 million dollar insurance policy on a spouse who is suing for divorce; or owning a for-profit health insurance company that makes more money just by denying claims; or loaning money on tricky terms to other countries so they must do business with your friends in your country and not their friends in their own country; or leaving a political office and the becoming a lobbyist; or being a CEO who makes $20 million a year no matter what happens; or out-sourcing jobs from your company's country to another country to increase profits for shareholders while decreasing employment at home. . . . Well, the list just goes on and on and on—*which is exactly why* Our Father counsels not to have any morals at all. Every moral principle observed becomes a *Moral Hazard* waiting to happen. Morality just adds hazards to the landscape. It's best to leave it alone.

**The Moral Majority,** *proper noun.* An American conservative political organization, now defunct, that was based on a fatally flawed assumption— because those who are moral are, we are proud so say, never the majority. (See *Fallen World.*)

**Mortgage,** *noun.* Conveyance of property to a creditor as security for the repayment of a debt. Based on the Latin word *mortuus*, meaning dead/death, and reflecting the fact that the *Mortgage* hounds you until your death—actually even after your death. **Sub-Prime Mortgage,** *noun.* Same as the above except that, rather than hounding you until death, it actually drives you to death and your country's financial institutions right along with you.

**Mozart, Wolfgang Amadeus,** *proper noun/name.* The greatest 18<sup>th</sup> century composer. His middle name *Amadeus* meant "beloved by God," but he wasn't. He made a pact with Our Father Below in order to be able to create music that was that good when he was that young. Unfortunately we lost the paperwork, so we can't back up our claim. But he was buried in a paupers' field grave—isn't that proof enough?

**Murder,** *noun and verb.* A highly effective and recommended form of conflict resolution.

**Murphy's Law,** *proper noun.* Murphy was an engineer for NASA when he discovered this important law in reference to highly engineered, complex systems: If something can go wrong, it will go wrong. This is a subtle variation on The Second Law of Thermodynamics; however, with the added devilish feature of the incompetence of humans and their hard working engineers, the principle captured in *Murphy's Law* rises to the realm of the truly sublime.

**Mystery,** *noun.* 1) A genre of the novel and drama in which the solving of a vicious and violent murder is turned into a voyeuristic leisure activity for consumers; 2) a religious truth unknowable except through divine revelation. Through the grace of Our Father Below and the wonders of the modern media, society now has a surplus of usage number 1 and a deficit of usage number 2.

**Mystic,** *noun.* A person who claims to attain insight into mysteries transcending ordinary human knowledge by immediate intuition and/or spiritual ecstasy—i.e., any member of a typical sophomore class at any New England College.

**Mysticism,** *noun.* A highly personal religion that can make one marvelously happy without the troublesome inconveniences of God, faith, commandments, sacraments, study, discipline, duty, thought, or reason.

**Myth,** *noun.* Some one else's religion, or any religion that has lost its punch. As in, for example, it is a myth that Prometheus gave fire to humans, or that the earth sits on top of a giant turtle, or that volcanoes are gods, or that Satan exists, etc. Myth is religion rendered safe for human consumption.

**Narcissist,** *noun.* A person who is a good judge of character.

**National Debt,** *noun & economic concept.* The gift of one generation to the next, and the next, and the next.

**Natura,** *proper noun.* The Goddess of Nature, the supreme deity of the late 20th century religion known as Environmentalism.

**Natural Death,** *noun.* The worst way to die, because hospitals and the practice of modern medicine do everything in their power to draw it out for as long as possible while at the same time making it as *unnatural* as possible.

**Natural,** *adjective.* A word that used to mean *coming from nature* and/or *in a natural state*; however, agro-business and the advertising industry have appropriated the word for their own higher purposes and now *Natural* has no real meaning at all, which is wonderfully devilish. (See *Organic*.)

**Natural Law,** *noun.* A highbrow term for the Holy Law of the Jungle. Examples: Dog eat dog; survival of the fittest; big fish eat little fish; natural selection via random mutation; Darwinism; *laissez faire* capitalism. *Natural Law* has quite an entirely different meaning for Catholic theologians, but they are sadly mistaken—and while they've been barking up the wrong tree our dog ate their dog.

**Nature,** *noun.* As Freud said, The principal task of civilization, in fact its reason for being, is to defend us against *Nature*.

**Nature Worship,** *proper noun.* A system of religion at the center of which is the supreme deification (and worship) of natural phenomena and forces. Previous to the 20$^{th}$ century, the Western World considered *Nature Worship* to be a prehistoric, early, formative stage of human religious development, which in most areas of the world went on to develop sequentially into pantheism, polytheism, and then into some form of proto-monotheism or monotheism. However, by the end of the 20$^{th}$ century, we can happily report that many people in the First World have returned to *Nature Worship* as their primary or only religion. (See *The Brights, Environmentalism*.)

**Nazareth,** *proper noun.* A small town in the north of present day Israel, the boyhood home of Jesus, Mary, and Joseph. As the Bible itself says: Has anything good ever come out of *Nazareth*? (*Gospel of John 1:46*)

**Necessity,** *noun.* Is the mother of invention . . . and the law . . . and the lawyers.

**Neo-Paganism,** *proper noun.* A progressive 20th century religious movement, embraced by the Nazis among others, that has steadfastly striven to bring humanity back to the good old days when animals, war prisoners, as well young boys and girls, were regularly sacrificed to a wonderful menagerie of fickle and demanding gods, ranging from Gaia to Zeus and from the goddess of grain to the god of the penis. (See *Priapus* and *Wicca*.)

**Neurosis,** *noun.* As brother Freud said: *Neurosis is a privilege of being human.*

**Neuterismo,** *noun.* A word that does not yet exist, but needs to be coined and put into use. *Neuterismo* is the only politically correct display of male sexuality that is permitted in the workplace, the classroom, public transportation, a public building, the sidewalk, or the bedroom—and permission must be obtained in writing first.

**New Age Movement (*aka* New Age Spirituality),** *proper noun.* A disorganized and non-centralized (unless southern California counts) religious movement that has become hugely popular since the 1970s, *New Age Spirituality* proudly takes its roots from astrology, channeling, Theosophy, Wicca, Hinduism, Taoism, Gnosticism, Paganism, Egoism, Narcissism, and perhaps a touch of Satanism—although we may be biased. As a manic mishmash of very old stuff tossed together to provide a smörgåsbord for the spiritually starved masses of the First World, the *New Age Movement* should more accurately be called the *Old Age Movement*, but that would not have quite the same ring to it.

**New Rome,** *proper noun.* When the Emperor Constantine the Great moved the capital of the Roman Empire from Rome to Byzantium in the early 300's, he rebuilt the old city and named it Constantinople. This city was soon also called *New Rome*, since everyone concerned understood that the real power, economic growth, and prestige of the Roman Empire was now centered in the Eastern Empire and not the Western. For 2,000 years since that time, various imperial regimes have styled themselves as the *New Rome*, including the king of England, Hitler, Mussolini, and most recently the empire of the United States. All around the world—with the notable exception of within Washington—the United States is widely considered to be, and is openly called, the *New Rome*. In as much as the Old Rome was the one that built the greatest empire on earth and executed the Son of God, Jesus Christ, Old Rome is a tough act to follow. But the United States is doing its best—with the help of its military, its banks, its corporations, its universities, and its MTV.

**New Testament,** *proper noun.* The second draft of the Bible. (See *Old Testament* and *Qur'an.*)

**New York Stock Exchange,** *proper noun.* The only gambling casino located in Manhattan.

**New World,** *proper noun.* The place where Europeans moved after they wore out their old world.

**New World Order,** *social-economic phrase.* The same old order—as set up and run by the Roman Empire and then the British Empire—except now ingenious Americans have given it a new, politically correct name.

**New York Times,** *proper noun/name.* A daily newspaper that claims to print "all the news that's fit to print," but actually prints all the news that fits . . . the needs of East Coast Liberal Democrats. (See *Wall Street Journal*.)

**The Next Generation,** *noun.* That round of births that follows the current one, the production of which was once thought to be a sacred, moral obligation, but now is considered unimportant because creating *The Next Generation* too often becomes too serious a burden on the current generation. (See *Birth Rate* and *Birth Control*.)

**Nietzsche, Friedrich,** *author, philosopher, theologian.* The greatest theologian of the western world, who wrote the immortal words: *"God is dead, God remains dead, and we have killed him. Who will wipe the blood off us? Is not the greatness of this deed too much for us? Must we ourselves not become gods simply to be worthy of it?"* He went insane and lived his later years in and out of mental institutions because he was too far ahead of his time. All true prophets are hounded until their death.

**Nihilist,** *noun.* A person who has achieved inner peace by the sublime realization that nothing is worth standing up for. Except perhaps dangling prepositions or the works of Friedrich Nietzsche.

.

**No,** *expletive.*   A negative used to express dissent, denial, or refusal; the most beautiful word in the English language.

ꞏ

**Noble Savage,** *noun.*   Jean Jacques Rouseau's profoundly misguided, romantic opinion to the contrary, the *Noble Savage* does not now, nor has ever, existed.  Our Father Below has considerable experience in this regard (both professional and personal) and it is his considered opinion that man is not, as Jean Jacques contended, "born good and made bad by society."  On the contrary, the good news is:  Man is born bad and made worse by society.  One must give credit where credit is due. (See *Original Sin.*)

**Nominalism,** *noun.*   A highly edifying, if frustrating, type of philosophy that has had a major impact on modern (and post-modern) thought, *Nominalism* stands for the position that: 1) general or abstract words of any sort never stand for actually existing entities of any sort; and 2) universals are nothing more than mere names (*nomens)* assigned by humans to abstractions invented by humans; and also further 3) each human assigns (*nominates*) those specific "universals" that answer to his own private perceptions—welcome to Los Angeles!  Consequently, the human mind has no warrant for establishing that a correspondence exists between the world of ideas and the world of reality—welcome to Hollywood!  This leaves humanity (along with its much touted higher consciousness) sliding down the proverbial slippery slope without the slightest shred of *terra firma* to grasp onto—a truly beautiful sight to see. And we are enjoying the show.

**Non Government Organizations (NGOs),** *noun.* Organizations that are not controlled by national governments and whose aims are generally to do good, due to the fact that national governments' aims are generally to do the opposite.

**Obedience,** *noun.*  Often the only handhold on a slippery slope.

**Obesity,** *noun.*  God's wrath upon the comfortable and the complaisant; it's worth taking note that *Obesity* is of epidemic proportions in the United States, a country that prides itself on being a so-called Christian nation.  (See *Malthus.*)

**Obey,** *verb.*  Man is born to *Obey.* That is why the antagonist is the true hero.

**Occam's Razor,** *proper noun.*  The absurdly misguided idea that the simplest answer is usually the right answer.  Go ahead, see how far *Occam's Razor* will get you in this Fallen World filled with politicians, lawyers, and statisticians.

**Off Shore,** *noun & adjective.*  Capitalism's tax-free, best-kept-secret-account Neverland, located in the Caribbean, now as always a haven for pirates of all sorts.  (See *Piracy.*)

**Old Age,** *noun.*  Is so contagious that everyone who lives long enough gets it.


**Old Testament,** *proper noun.*  The first draft of the Bible.  (See *New Testament* and *Qur'an.)*


**Opportunity,** *noun.*  Knocks only once—if that.


**Optimist,** *noun.*  An unfortunate person who is never able to appreciate the sublime beauty of defeat.


**Organic,** *adjective.*  A word that had to be invented to replace the word *natural* due to verbal pollution purposely dumped onto the word *natural* by the advertising industry.  (See *Natural.*)


**Organic Farming,** *noun.*  Farming based on a lot of natural, healthy bullshit, rather than on a lot of unnatural, unhealthy bullshit.  (See *Chemical Weapons.*)


**Orgasm,** *noun.*  The central sacrament of Secular Humanism.  (See *Sacrament.*)

**The Orient, Orientalism,** *noun.* From the Latin *oriens*, meaning east. In the old days of the Holy Roman Empire, the *Orient* originally meant, basically, all things east of Jerusalem—which were held to be places and peoples unknown, unsavory, untrustworthy, and unwholesome. *Orientalism* is a modern mindset in the Western First World which holds that all places and peoples east of Jerusalem are unknown, unsavory, untrustworthy, and unwholesome.

**Original Intent,** *noun & legal term.* This is a term that refers to the original ideas and intentions of the original framers of the U. S. constitution. Basing an argument or decision on *Original Intent* means that the framers' intention way back then just happens, fortunately, to agree with what modern constitutional lawyers intend the framers' words to mean right now, at least for now, as long as five of nine Supreme Court judges intentionally decide that it's OK. (Note: not to be confused with *Original Sin,* despite the similarities.)

**Original Sin,** *noun.* A Christian theological concept which holds that all humans are born with a wondrous, innate tendency toward evil, which has been handed down consistently generation to generation from Adam and Eve themselves. Anyone who has lived through parenting a teenager should have no difficulty understanding the concept of *Original Sin*.   What further proof could be needed of Our Father Below's earthly dominion? *Q.E.D.*

**An Original Thought,** *noun.*   Always a good thing never to have.

**Other People's Money,** *noun, business term.*   The best kind of money to use . . . or lose.

**Orthodoxy, Heterodoxy,** *nouns, religious terms.* As Bishop Warburton said to Lord Sandwich: *Orthodoxy* is my doxy; *heterodoxy* is another man's doxy.

**The Our Father Below** (*aka* **Pater Noster Infernus**)**,** *prayer.*   "Our Father Below who art in hell, harrowing be thy name.  Thy kingdom has come, thy will is being done on earth as it is in hell. Give us this day our daily brandy, and never forgive us our trespasses, as we never forgive those who trespass against us.  Lead us into every temptation through the wonders of modern advertising, and deliver us to evil."

**Our Lady of Guadalupe,** *proper noun.*   Another name for the highly beloved Aztec goddess Tonantzin (*"Our Holy Mother"*), who miraculously appeared to a humble Indian peasant named Juan Diego on Dec. 9, 1531, as he was walking slightly north of the current Mexico City, crossing the hill of Tepeyac where there had been an ancient temple of the goddess—which had been demolished by the Spanish in their zeal for the way of The Enemy. Catholic priests at the time immediately appropriated this appearance as a visitation from the Blessed Virgin Mary, calling her *Our Lady of Guadalupe,* and they were probably the ones who concocted the miraculous painting on Juan Diego's cape to prove it—which is on display to this day in the Basilica of Guadalupe, visited by millions of devout pilgrims each year. Anthropologists call this an example of religious syncretism, but we call it, at the very least, a case of mistaken identity or, at the worst, a serious case of copyright infringement.


**Out-Source,** *verb.* A business term in late 20th century capitalism for the action of taking away work from workers who are paid a decent wage in order to give the work to workers who are paid an indecent wage. Our Father Below is always in favor of any indecency, however small or large.

**Pace of Life,** *noun.* From our point of view, the faster the better.

**Paganism,** *noun.* A superior form of ancient religion that allows plenty of room for Our Father Below to move around in total freedom. (See *Progressive Christianity.*)

**Pain and Suffering,** *nouns.* The wages of doing good.

**Pandemonium,** *proper noun.* In his epic poem about Lucifer, *Paradise Lost,* Milton identified *Pandemonium* as the capital of Hell. Literally meaning *"Place of All Demons"* ( < Greek *pan + daimon*); it is known in modern times as New York City, commemorated by the naming of a midtown West Side neighborhood as *Hell's Kitchen.*

**Partial Truth,** *noun.* Remember, never be *Partial* to the *Truth*—and never resort to a *Partial Truth* when a *total falsehood* could do. (See *Half Truth.*)

**Pascal, Pascal's Wager,** *proper nouns.* Blaise *Pascal* was an important French philosopher and mathematician who lived in the 17$^{th}$ century. He ruminated on the quandary as to why, in an Age of Science and Reason, should a person believe in God and an afterlife. He arrived at a carefully considered conclusion that has come to be called *Pascal's Wager.* Since one has the choice to believe or not to believe, *Pascal* asked which is the more logical choice (or wager)*: A)* On the one hand, if one has chosen to believe, but there is no God nor afterlife, then one has simply chosen the wrong side of a metaphysical and academic question—and there will be no negative impacts to follow. Or, *B)* On the other hand, if there is God and afterlife, and one has chosen to reject both God and afterlife, then one has chosen the wrong side of a serious life-and-death issue—and there will be negative impacts to follow. As they old saying goes, There'll be hell to pay. This leads to the simple logical extension: It is better to live as if God exists rather than live as if God does not exist. *Pascal's Wager* points toward the best bet in the game at hand. Fortunately for The Cause of Our Father Below, most people don't know about *Pascal's Wager,* just as most people are bad at cards—and, the best part, gamblers tend to forget that the house always wins.


**Passion,** *proper noun.* In the modern Secular Age, *Passion* used as a proper noun has two meanings: 1) the name of a well known women's perfume; 2) the name of the final hours of the suffering of Jesus Christ on the cross. *Question*: Is nothing sacred? *Answer*: No.

**Patriarchy,** *noun.* An out-dated and misogynistic form of social organization whereby the father is the ultimate authority in the family and descent is reckoned through the male line, slowly but steadily being abandoned in the Western First World. (See *Matriarchy*.)

**Patriotism,** *noun.* The last refuge of a scoundrel, the first refuge of a sycophant, the first and last refuge of a politician.

**Peace,** *noun.* A forever unattainable state of affairs between factions of mankind, achieved momentarily now and again here and there solely for the purpose of being able to plan further and more deadly forms of war.

**Peace Force,** *noun.* An unintentional oxymoron coined by military intelligence.

**Peaceful Coexistence,** *noun.* An oxymoron accepted by the hopelessly naive.

**Peacekeeper Missile,** *noun.*  A deadly oxymoron that never keeps the peace.


**Peacemakers,** *noun.*  Blessed are the peacemakers for they always fail.


**Peaceable Kingdom,** *noun.*  Something that exists only in the school of Romantic painting.


**The People of the Book,** *proper noun.*  This is a phrase that collectively identifies the three monotheisms Judaism, Christianity, and Islam—due to the fact that each is based on *The Book* and this *Book* (or *Books*) for Christians and Muslims, includes materials that, at least supposedly, overlap and/or follow each other.  All three share a common origin, at least in theory, with the the Torah of the Jews, known to Christians as the Old Testament. However, Christians read the Old Testament somewhat differently than the Jews did and do— and Christians believe fervently that their reading of *The Book* is the only correct one.  Likewise, Muslims' approach to the Old and New Testaments, as explained in their *Book* the Qur'an, is different from the way either Jews or Christians read *The Book*—and Muslim's believe fervently that their reading of *The Book* is the only correct one.  Jews read the Torah in their own way, and Jews fervently believe their reading of *The Book* is the only correct one, not caring fig for how Christians and Muslims read it. So they all are *"The People of the Book"* in the specific sense that they are the people who agree to disagree about *The Book.*

**Perfection,** *noun.* Even *Perfection* is not perfect.

**Person,** *noun.* The second\* most controversial word in the English language—and several other languages as well. How does one define what is a *Person*? Under United States law, for example, a corporation is a *Person,* while an embryo is not a *Person.* Or, who has more rights under the law—a *Corporate Person* or a human *Person*? And just to add to the confusion, in French the word for "nobody" is *Personne.* (\*See *Embryo.*)

**Pessimist,** *noun.* A realist without much tact.

**Piety,** *noun.* The other side of hypocrisy, composing the two pillars of all religions.

**Pimp,** *noun.* A member of the management class in a very old profession.

**Piracy,** *noun.* The ultimate *Free Market* business.

**Plagiarize,** *verb.*  To write a college research paper in a hurry.

**Plague,** *noun and verb.*  A superior and natural method of periodically cleansing the human race and improving the gene pool. Unfortunately for all concerned, modern medicine is putting *Plagues* out of business—and at the end of the day there'll be Hell to pay.

**Plastic Surgery,** *noun.*  An elective medical procedure to make what's on the outside look better than what's on the inside—in light of the human condition and original sin this is always a good idea.

**Platonic Love,** *proper noun.*  Doesn't exist, never has. An artificially invented concept of a certain supposedly noble type of love that purportedly excluded and/or attempted to rise above sexual relations. The term *Platonic Love* was coined by a bunch of old, stodgy, homophobic non-Greek speaking professors who seriously misread the ancient philosopher Plato some two thousand plus years after his death. Plato in actuality had written an explicit defense of how and why men's sexual relations with young boys (or the sublimated desire thereof) was always superior to consensual sexual relations between an adult man and woman—an opinion he shared with most of his honorable and open minded fellow male citizens of Athens. Those were exemplary days for non-discrimination on the basis of sexual orientation, unfortunately brought to a tragic end by the pernicious spread of Christianity.

**Pleasure,** *noun.*   Our brother Epicurus said it very well: *Pleasure* is the beginning and end of the good life.   Our Father Below heartily recommends this principle and is delighted to see its acceptance growing so steadily again around the world.

**Pluralism,** *noun.*   A late 20th century school of enlightened philosophy and social theory which holds that there are now any number of mutually contradictory sets of cultural guidelines held by people—existing and operating not only around the planet, but also increasingly within a given country or a given city.   Further, that attempts to meld and reshape these various cultural value sets into one inclusive culture are misguided, manipulative, and doomed to fail.   In light of the Second Law of Thermodynamics, this is probably (and fortunately) correct.   Chaos is always good and one set of purportedly moral values is just as good as another.

**Political Correctness,** *noun.*   A highly valued form of Post-Modern social grace, according to which no sensitive or crucial issues concerning ethics, morality, or religion are allowed to be discussed with an open mind in polite society.

**Politician,** *noun.* A term for some one who makes his living in the world's second* oldest profession via bribes and kick backs. (*See *Prostitution.*)


**Political Appointee,** *noun.* *A* politician in sheep's clothing. (See *Lobbyist.*)


**Political Party,** *noun.* As our brother Swift noticed: A *Political Party* exploits the madness of many for the benefit of the few.


**Politics,** *noun.* The dark art of the possible in a fallen world. And as Disraeli said: In *Politics* nothing is contemptible.


**Poll,** *noun.* A process, usually expensive, whereby a certain number of people are asked leading questions, which are worded in a particular way in order to obtain a particular result, so that said result supports the assumptions, values, and hypotheses of the those who paid for the *Poll* in the first place. (See *Statistician.*)


**Pollyanna,** *noun.* A person suffering from an excessively and blindly optimistic outlook usually caused by youth, stupidity, or a genetic flaw.

**Polygamy,** *noun.*   The natural, preferred, most happy, and most efficient form of marital relations between men and women, with an ancient, well established pedigree.   Due to the hegemonic influence of the Judeo-Christian religious tradition, *Polygamy* is now illegal or heavily discriminated against almost everywhere; however, it is slowly making a return to favor through the tireless efforts of select groups of enlightened Mormons and Muslims.  Onward and upward.

**Polytheism,** *noun.*   The next best thing to atheism. Pantheism is even better.

**Polyglot,** *noun.*   Some one who needlessly persists in speaking many languages instead of just speaking English.

**Pope, Pontiff,** *proper noun.*   The Bishop of Rome, the head of the Catholic Church, usurper of the ancient Roman title *Pontifex Maximus* (Supreme Pontiff), which had been reserved for the Supreme Priest of the pagan Roman state religion, going back some 700 years before the birth of Jesus. What can we say that hasn't already been said?  Over the last two thousand years, there have been a few good ones who had any number of children and practiced graft, greed, simony, and nepotism on epic proportions, but on the whole a damn tough bunch of captains for The Enemy's ship of state.

167

**Poor in Spirit,** *Biblical phrase.* "Blessed are the poor in spirit...." Yes, stop right there—that's our point.

**Pork,** *noun.* Jews avoid it; politicians crave it.

**Pope Pius XII,** *proper noun/name.* Born Eugenio Pacelli of an old aristocratic Roman family, *Pope Pius XII* (1939-1958) was one of the most controversial popes in history. On account of his actions toward the Jews during WWII, he was considered saintly by many Jews and Catholics; but now, on account or in spite of those very same actions, he is considered demonic by many who are neither Jews nor Catholics. Our Father Below has no opinion on *Pope Pius XII*, due to the highly unfortunate fact that they have never met—and it looks like they never will.

**Popularity,** *noun.* Is to treacherousness as condemnation is to truthfulness.

**Pornography,** *noun.* A free speech right of the *Sexual Revolution,* now protected by the United States constitution.

**Positive Thinking,** *noun.* The manifestly absurd idea that humans can better their lives and themselves in their Fallen World simply by changing their way of thinking about themselves and their world. This foolhardy enterprise was put forth with a vengeance by a virulently anti-Catholic, Protestant preacher named Dr. Norman Vincent Peale. His book *The Power of Positive Thinking*, published in 1952, remained on the New York Times bestseller list for over three years, selling many millions of copies in many languages. And just look at how much better the world has become since 1952. (See *Positivism* and *Fallen World.*)

**Positivism, Logical Positivism,** *proper noun.* A type of philosophy that is based on the rejection of metaphysics and/or transcendence to any higher plain and holds that the only real and authentic knowledge is that which is based on the authority of sense experience and scientific experiment coupled with human reason. Through an impressive feat of mental acrobatics, August Comte and his 19th and 20th century followers, after totally rejecting any transcendent truth as something one can be *Positive* about, then named their philosophy *Positivism*. In the current Secular Age most sensible, well educated people are positive that *Positivism* is positively right and that *Logical Positivism* is even more positively right—and that's positively grand as far as Our Father is concerned.

**Post-Modernism,** *noun.*   A term for the latest, most elegant and culminating stage of philosophy, achieved in the latter 20$^{th}$ century, by which it is held that no unchanging truths or standards for anything exist or have ever existed, and that frames of reference to any all-encompassing modes of thought and judgment are nothing but arbitrary and vacuous human constructs.   Post-Modern *Memo* to all the world's religions: May you Rest In Peace and Our Father Below have no mercy on your souls—which probably don't exist anyway. (See *Sophistry.*)

**Pragmatism,** *proper noun.*   A school of 20$^{th}$ century philosophy based on the precept that the validity of all values and concepts is to be determined solely by those values' and concepts' practicality and practical consequences. This leads to the happy result that truth is equated with whatever works and is practical—so everyone can relax since there's no such thing as an inconvenient truth.   Our Father Below couldn't have said it better himself.

**Pray,** *verb.*   An antiquated, pointless activity whereby humans used to think they could bring themselves in some way closer to their God. Fortunately more and more are realizing that nothing comes of it—after all, as the saying goes, What's in it for me?   (See *Deafening Silence.*)

**Preemptive War,** *noun.* A wonderful idea whose day has returned. (See *Terrorism.*)

**Priapus,** *proper noun.* The ancient Roman god of the erect penis, now worshiped under the name Viagra.

**Pride,** *noun.* That highest of human virtues that goes right up to just before a fall.

**Prime Mover (First Cause),** *proper noun.* This is a term that all devout atheists believed was finally put out of business in the 20$^{th}$ century, with the scientific community's acceptance of a Steady State Model for the universe and the Evolutionary Model for life forms. *Prime Mover* and *First Cause* are terms to refer simply to that which logically must have come before the origin of the universe—that which put things in motion and/or caused things to come into existence. It was pretty easy to get rid of these words when the science folks said the universe did not in fact have a beginning, it just is and has always been in a "Steady State", so it never had any need for, nor was there any room for, a *Prime Mover* or *First Cause* of any sort. Then (poof!) by the end of the 20$^{th}$ century other science folks have proven beyond a doubt that the universe did, in fact, have a beginning and it was about 15 billion years ago (give or take a half a billion). Background radiation and various other observations confirm this clearly.  So now the old *Prime Mover* or *First Cause* is right back center stage, going under the new name of *The Initial Singularity*.  It's not as easy to kick The Enemy out of his own house as your average, run-of-the-mill atheist might think.  As Our (multi-lingual) Father Below is fond of saying:  *"Plus ca change, plus c'est la meme chose."*  (See *Steady State.*)

**Principal (Principle),** *noun & adjective.*  The main, initial investment into a money market account or trust fund, from which the monthly income (profit) is derived.  As in, for example, one well dressed but scantily clad trust funderette saying to another: "Well, we may be turning tricks on 41st Street, but at least we haven't sacrificed our *Principals*."  The word *Principle* is just a misspelling of *Principal*.

**Prison,** *noun.*  In the U.S. a low cost, minimal service hotel with a weight room and better health care (free of charge) than most citizens have while living on the outside.  Who says crime doesn't pay?

**Private School,** *noun.*  A public school in England.  (See *Public School.*)

***Pro Bono (Pro Bono Publico),*** *legal term.*  From the Latin *pro* (in favor of) + *bono* (good), meaning "for the public good." This refers to the 2 uncompensated hours per week corporate lawyers devote to bettering the welfare of society (*pro bono publico*), as distinct from the 70 highly over compensated hours they devote to undermining the welfare of society.

**Procrastination,** *noun.* The fine art, indicative of good character, of never doing today what can be put off till tomorrow, indicating a very healthy and positive attitude toward one's future. From the Latin *pro* (in favor of) + *cras* (tomorrow).

**Procrastinator,** *noun.* A member of the United States Congress.

**Progressive Christianity**, *noun.* A superior form of 20$^{th}$ century religion that allows plenty of room for Our Father Below to move around in total freedom. (See *Paganism.*)

**Proletariat,** *noun.* Out dated, politically incorrect term for the least expensive work force that can be found anywhere on earth, or can be made to move anywhere on earth, for the benefit of the owners of the means of production. Often to be found living in substandard housing without security, windows, or doors. (See *Bourgeoisie.*)

**Prophet,** *noun.*   Some one who sees what's coming, tries to tell everybody, and then most likely is killed as thanks for his efforts.

**Propaganda,** *noun.*   When a government one dislikes gives out misinformation about its own activities, it is called *Propaganda*; when a government one likes gives out misinformation about its own activities, it is called Public Relations. (See *Manufactured Consent.*)

**Prostitution,** *noun.*   The world's oldest profession and perhaps the only totally honest relation between the sexes.   Par for the course for humanity, *Prostitution* is illegal and persecuted almost always and almost everywhere—except in a few enlightened places dear to Our Father Below, such as Nevada and Amsterdam and certain brownstones on the Upper East Side of Manhattan.

**Proselytize,** *verb.*   When Christians and Muslims do it, it's considered saintly; when we do it, it's considered devilish.

**Protestant Reformation,** *proper noun.*   A movement of protest against the Catholic Church, begun in Germany by a rabid anti-Semite who bore the name Luther, which almost rhymes with Lucifer. Divide and conquer, as they say.   It always works.

**Protestant Work Ethic,** *sociological & religious term.* The firmly held conviction held by certain self-righteous and self-satisfied Protestants that they work harder and better and smarter and saintlier than anyone else on earth, thereby proving that they are predestined and chosen by God to rule the world and be rewarded in Heaven. And Our Father loves them for it. Pride is the greatest of virtues.

**Provincetown (Massachusetts),** *proper noun.* San Francisco back East. If you don't get it, that's OK.

**Psychologist, Psychiatrist,** *noun.* A 20th century invention to replace the function of a good (or even a bad) priest. A psychologist, however, is by far the lesser of two evils, since he will leave the Enemy and His issues of good and evil based on Divine Revelation out of the discussion. A *Psychiatrist* is the same thing, except even better because he can and will prescribe Psychotropic Drugs.

**Psychopath, Psychopathic Personality,** *noun, psychological and legal term.* A *Psychopathic Person* is a person whose personality persistently evidences: strong tendencies toward amoral, anti-social behavior; lack of an ability to understand, give, or receive love and affection; lack of an ability to differentiate right from wrong; lack of an ability to establish meaningful relationships; and a constant egocentricity. So a *Psychopathic Person* is either a devilishly dysfunctional human person or a perfectly performing corporation—always remember that a corporation is, after all, a *Person* under United States law. (See *Corporate Personhood.*)

**Psychotropic Drugs,** *noun.* Legal and illegal chemicals ingested by humans in order to assist them in making the psychological and spiritual adjustments needed to cope with the overwhelming and incessant stresses of life in advanced, post-industrial societies of the Western World's Post-Modern, secular age—thereby helping toward the ultimate glorious fulfillment of Our Father's dominion on earth.

**Public School,** *noun.* A private school in England. (See *Private School.*)

**Punitive Justice,** *noun.* A type legal jurisprudence by which transgressors of the law are punished in proportion to their transgressions. While *Punitive Justice* may be central in all systems of Secular Law, in the enlightened Secular Age of today *Punitive Justice* has been declared inadmissible and overly primitive in Sacred Law. (Ergo: Not only does Hell not exist, there's not even any reason for Hell to exist; it just isn't allowed, so relax.)

***Q.E.D., Quod Erat Demonstrandum,*** *Latin expression used in logic.* Meaning *that which was to be demonstrated has been demonstrated.* Highly useful in speaking with some one who has little Latin and less Greek when you want to finish your argument in a very petty and patronizing way. (*Ergo: Used often in this text.*)

**Quality of Life,** *noun.* Hopeless and miserable.

**Quantitative Analysis**, *noun.* The statistical and numerical form of empirical analysis that has sought to deny and has succeeded in denying any validity to qualitative analysis. If truth cannot be quantified numerically and statistically then it is simply no longer truth. This leads to the happy state of affairs where well educated people know the price of everything and the value of nothing.

**Quantum Mechanics,** *proper noun.* A form of contemporary physics quite antithetical to materialist philosophy; but fortunately for Our Father's

177

Cause very few have taken the trouble to understand *Quantum Mechanics,* so the Materialists are still allowed to hold the floor—at least in the sacred halls of secular academia. (See *E = MC squared.*)

**Quit,** *verb.* To stop striving to achieve something; the most important verb in the English language.

**Quid Pro Quo,** *Latin phrase, legal concept.* "This on account of that." Something that those in service to The Cause of Our Father Below should think very carefully about. (See *Punitive Justice.*)

**Qur'an** (*aka* **Quran, Koran),** *proper noun.* The third draft of the Bible. (See *Old Testament* and *New Testament.)*

# R

**Ayn Rand,** *proper noun, pen name.* Well known mid-20<sup>th</sup> century Russian-born American author, now the center of a religious cult. She has become Our Blessed Lady of Wall Street and the Patron Saint of Individualism and unbridled, free market capitalism. As evidenced by the well known investment bankers' universal prayer for intercession: "Hail, Ayn, Full of Greed, Our Father is with thee, blessed art thou among women and blessed is the fruit of thy pen, *The Fountainhead.* Holy Ayn, Mother of Gold, pray for us sinners now and at the hour of our bankruptcy."

**Race,** *noun.* A socially constructed, imaginary concept invented by Europeans in order to convince themselves and others that the European *Race* was the superior one. An absolutely crazy idea, but when combined with a potent mixture of Social Darwinism it worked like a charm. Bravo.

**Race Relations,** *noun.* The art and science of subtly keeping one's own race on top while keeping the other races on the bottom.

179

**Random Mutation,** *noun.* Our Father's Grand Plan being carried out on earth, especially in biology departments. (See *Evolution, Darwin, Darwinism.*)

**Read,** *verb.* A dangerous activity once performed by humans whereby they could access the wisdom of the ancients and make informed decisions regarding themselves and their various forms of self governance. Fortunately, the tendency for indulging in this vice is passing away.

**Real Estate,** *noun.* Physical property (i.e. land and buildings) in the United States that used to belong to human persons prior to the 21$^{st}$ century, but now belongs to banks, large insurance companies, and *Corporate Persons.*

**Reason,** *noun.* The most useful tool on Our Father's rack; since humans tend to forget that they are not perfect, their less-than-perfect faculty of *Reason* can easily convince them of countless errors, leading them wondrously down the path toward the welcoming arms of Our Father Below.

**Recreational Sex,** *noun.* Is there any other kind? (See *Sex.*)

**Religion,** *noun.* Ambrose Bierce got this one half right: "The daughter of Hope and Fear, explaining to Ignorance the nature of the Unknowable." Fortunately for our Father's Cause, more and more institutions of learning in the formerly Christian First World are banishing *Religion* from their offerings—or, even better still, religion may be studied only as an item of antique curiosity, safely relegated to a quarantined place, kept at a distance, locked away within historical context. Progress marches on. (See *Harvard Divinity School.*)

**Relativism,** *noun.* The manifestly obvious and valid philosophical theory that all criteria and judgments are deemed *Relative*, always varying with individuals and their environments. Truth is arrived at by vote, whether the voters realize it or not. Absolute truth is absolutely unattainable and, more importantly, absolutely unnecessary. As in, "Hey, dude, it's all *Relative* . . . so whatever."

**Religious Freedom,** *proper noun.* In Western Europe, the United States, and Canada the right to *Religious Freedom* means that one has the right to one's religion, so long as one's religion doesn't have any rights.

**Repressed Memory Syndrome,** *proper noun & psychological term.* A wonderfully diabolical psychological concept, now unfortunately widely discredited, that was invented by a group of well-meaning psychologists who had apparently never read a single word of Sigmund Freud; who had apparently never heard of the insightful concepts of Original Sin or the Fallen State of man; and who fervently believed that every person's memories, especially children's memories, are always perfectly pure, pristine, and never wrong—and that an interviewer couldn't possibly, willfully or not, ever influence another person's recollections. (How on earth do experts come up with this stuff? Do they get PhDs to come up with this stuff? Well, we applaud them fervently for coming up with it.)

**Republican,** *proper noun.* A politician who protects interests of corporate persons and human persons in that order, but running almost neck and neck. (See *Democrat,* and *Corporate Personhood.*)

**Resignation,** *noun.* One of the most noble of human character traits.

**Respect for Life, Sanctity of Life,** *noun and religious concept.* The counter-intuitive idea that all human life is sacred to God—a very inconvenient proposition, stubbornly held onto by the Catholic Church. We have to admit, however, in support of this idea one could pose a very vexing question: Unless all human life were sacred to God, why would He allow atheists, sinners, secular humanists, and most college professors to go on living?

**Responsibility,** *noun.* The only thing one should never take.

**Revolution,** *noun.* The People's rapid and usually violent overthrow of one set of abusive tyrants in order to make themselves subjects of a new set of abusive tyrants. As in the French *Revolution*, the Industrial *Revolution*, the Computer *Revolution*, and the Sexual *Revolution*.

**Right,** *adjective and proper noun.* The one that doesn't know what the left one is doing—in politics as in life.

**Right to Bear Arms**, *legal phrase.* Now there's a human *Right* we stand behind. (See *Human Rights.*)

**Right to Life,** *noun, political-religious expression.* This phrase refers to a tenet held by many denominations of Christianity and by all denominations of Islam, which asserts that all human life is sacred to God and must be preserved and protected in all its stages from natural conception until natural death—granted, thanks to the wonders of modern medicine, "natural conception" and "natural death" are increasingly hard to pin down. But Our Father Below holds that this tenet is at best troublesome and at worst downright dangerous. If there is a *Right to Life*, what comes next? The *Right* to human rights? The *Right* to religious freedom? The *Right* to have water or food? The *Right* to receive an education? The *Right* to have health care? The *Right* to vote? The *Right* to a fair trial? On the contrary, Our Father Below asserts that the so-called *Right to Life*, just like all co-called *Rights,* is not a *Right* at all but a privilege—a privilege enjoyed by those who are already here and granted by them (at their discretion) to those who may or may not (also at their discretion) arrive after them.

**Robert's Rules of Order,** *proper noun.* The only sacred book that is allowed to provide any form of higher order in Congress or Parliament.

**Roman Alphabet,** *proper noun.* The only alphabet used on every continent on earth and on the moon; written proof of the ongoing impact of the great, voracious, vicious, and victorious Roman Empire. (See *Romance Languages.*)

**Romance Languages,** *proper noun.* About half the people on the planet speak a *Romance Language* as either their first or second language. *Romance*

*Languages* are those languages that are the direct descendants of the ancient Latin language used in Rome and much of its Empire, but the only one that's truly *Romantic* is Italian—at least according to Italians (and according to many young American tourists).

**Romance Novel,** *noun.*   A genre of fantasy fiction, written for women by women, based the idea that there are straight men who care about flowers, place settings, dancing, and whispering sweet nothings by candlelight prior to having passionate, out of control, and (barely) consensual sex.

**Rome,** *proper noun.*   A large European city that once had a great, pagan past as the seat of the world's greatest empire, but it has been going downhill ever since.

**Rumor,** *noun.*   The closest friend of truth when one has no idea what the truth is.

# S

**Sabbath,** *noun.* Taken from religious doctrine and tradition, the establishment of one day each week to be free from work in order to be free for shopping.

**Sacrament,** *noun.* From the Latin *sacare* (to devote) + *mentum* (-ment), meaning literally "devotion-ment." In Christian tradition and doctrine, a *Sacrament* is a visible sign instituted by Jesus to both symbolize and confer grace. Protestantism observes two *Sacraments:* Baptism and the Lord's Supper. Catholicism observes seven *Sacraments:* Baptism, Confirmation, the Eucharist, Matrimony, Penance, Holy Orders, and Extreme Unction at death. Modern Secular Humanism observes five *Sacraments:* Empiricism, Freedom, Orgasm, Abortion, and Divorce.

**Sacred Law,** *proper noun.* There is no longer any such thing. But when there was, *Sacred Law* was believed to be a set of unchanging laws and values which originated from a source that transcended mankind's transient perspective and was revealed to man through one or another form of Divine

Revelation. Fortunately for Our Cause, enlightened humans now know better.

**SAD,** *abbreviation, medical term.* Acronym for the psychological condition named Seasonal Affective Disorder, also for the psychological condition known as Sensible Acceptance of Defeat.

**Sadism,** *noun.* The almost universal and always admirable human tendency to receive pleasure from inflicting pain upon another.

**Sadomasochism,** *noun.* 1) The best of both worlds; 2) two wrongs do make a right; 3) a sexual preference now designated as a civil right and fully protected by the constitutions of Canada, the European Union, and the United States.

**Safe for Democracy,** *diplomatic expression.* A slip of the tongue or a journalist's error. What he thought he said was, "Make the world safe for plutocracy."

**Saint,** *noun.* A dead sinner with a make-over done at the world's most exclusive salon in Vatican City.

**Saint Peter's,** *proper noun.* A structure that was originally built by the pagan, opportunist, convert Emperor Constantine, who in the process desecrated 'the beautiful Circus of Nero. It has now become the most visited church of The Enemy anywhere on the face of the earth. (See *Circus of Nero.*)


**Same Sex Marriage,** *noun, legal phrase.* A late 20$^{th}$ century re-definition of the word *marriage,* introduced in some parts of Europe and North America. Prior to the third millennium in all cultures in all locations and times the term *Marriage* (in whatever language) has referred to an institution whereby a man and a woman (or in rare instances more than one man or one woman) formed a union primarily for the socially constructive purpose of procreating the next generation of the species. Except for a few locations in Europe and North America, the word *Marriage* still carries this meaning. However, with the re-definition of sex and gender among the affluent, along with technological advances in birth control and artificial insemination available to them, *Marriage* for enlightened residents of the First World has been redefined as an institution that has nothing to do with procreation. For some strange reason, assuredly unrelated, the birth and fertility rates among these enlightened First World residents is uniformly falling below replacement level—that is, the procreation needed to sustain a stable population level is not happening. In light of this most happy turn of events, *Same Sex Marriage* is a logical step and a great idea—all that remains is to figure out a way to get around that inconvenient procreation-through-sexual-reproduction thing that has been universal to all higher life forms for so many millions of years. (See *Sexual Reproduction.*)

**SAT,** *abbreviation, educational term.* Acronym for "Scholastic Aptitude Test," also for "Silly Asinine Test." The SAT is a widely used multiple choice examination, carefully designed by a bunch of college Education Departments, to assess high school students' aptitude for being slightly better than average under-achievers (but far better than average test-takers) during their college years, thereby predicting that they will likely remain slightly better than average under-achievers for the remainder of their mundane, under acheiving lives.

**Satan,** *proper noun/name.* An antiquated mythological figure who was purported to be the arch enemy of God; the fallen angel, Lucifer, thrown out of heaven with his co-conspirators; as of the 20th century all enlightened humans know that he doesn't exist. *Satan* derives from the Hebrew word for "adversary". (See *Lucifer, Antagonist.*)

**Satanists,** *noun.* God's loyal opposition.

**Satellite,** *noun.* A mobile, electronic device sent up very high in order to send down very low culture.

**Satire,** *noun.* Is the highest form of flattery.

**Scatological Speech,** *noun.* The fine art of using language in a musical, metaphorical, metaphysical, and mischievous way.

**Science,** *noun.* Ah, yes . . . the Devil is in the details, as the saying goes.

**Scientology,** *noun.* See *Science* and multiply by one hundred—but it claims to be a religion.

**Scruple,** *noun.* A moral or ethical principle that acts as a restraining force to inhibit certain actions. From the Latin *scrupulus*, meaning a small, rough pebble. And like getting rid of a pebble in your shoe, it's best just to get rid of *Scruples*.

**Secretary of Defense,** *proper noun.* Used to be called the Secretary of War, so that ought to give you some idea—enough said. (See *Doublespeak.*)

**Second Law of Thermodynamics,** *proper noun.* The physical law that can be stated as follows: In any isolated system in our universe the entropy (i.e., disorder) never decreases. Daily, absolute proof of the dominion of Our Father Below and that his will is in harmony with the cosmos.

**Secular, Secular Age,** *adjective, noun.* An age focused on worldly things and/or on things that are *not* regarded as religious, spiritual, or sacred. A *Secular Age* is an age, such as the present in Europe and parts of the United States, that is entirely concerned with worldly, material things and disregards all that is religious or sacred—unless a religious holiday can be turned into an opportunity for increased shopping. Fortunately for The Cause of Our Father, the Second Law of Thermodynamics (see above) seems to work in favor of *Secular Ages.*

**Secular Humanism,** *noun.* A mode of thought or action in which human interests, values, achievement, and dignity are given the central place, without recourse to or room for religious values, traditions, or rites. Despite the fact that *Humanism* was an invention of Catholic scholars in the European Renaissance, in the 20th century philosophers and scholars became convinced that one can have a better *Humanism* by completely detaching it from its Christian roots; and thereby giving it a new name: *Secular Humanism.* Surely they were right, because look at the glorious results achieved in Nazi Germany, Fascist Italy, Communist Russia, Red China, and North Korea—all truly outstanding examples of the advances that unbridled *Secular Humanism* can accomplish in improving upon humanity, once *Humanism* is freed from the out dated moral shackles of religion and its supposedly transcendent truths.

**Secular Humanist,** *noun.* A college professor anywhere in the northeastern United States, even at Notre Dame, in the late 20$^{th}$ or early 21$^{st}$ century.

**Secular Law,** *proper noun.* Law determined by a vote and by what works; has replaced *Sacred Law* in all enlightened societies. (See *Pragmatism.*)

**Secular Values,** *noun.* A contradiction in terms, but nonetheless *Secular Values* are those sets of values that have been and can be agreed upon by a majority vote of the populace, the legislature, the Supreme Court, or of college and university faculties along with their respective student assemblies—or values perhaps agreed upon by one's condominium or block association, or by the United Nations or the World Trade Organization. If this sounds like it might result in some very serious contradictions and self-serving decisions, that's because it does result in some very serious contradictions and self-serving decisions.

**Secularism,** *noun.* The highest and most advanced form of social systems, arrived at during the 20$^{th}$ century in Western Europe, Canada, Australia, the United States, the Soviet Union, Cuba, and the People's Republic of China, whereby it is agreed that political, governmental, and societal affairs should be conducted in a way that rejects and avoids any and all forms of religious values, faith, worship, or theology. Similarly, public education and civil law must be conducted without the introduction of any religious precepts or elements. And further, religious institutions should be closed and their personnel put out of work. Our Father Below couldn't have done it better himself.

**Seculments,** *noun.* Visible, outward signs in the material world of the invisible, inward victory of the secular over the sacred, made possible through the grace of Our Father Below. Such as: expensive cars, designer jeans, McMansions, breast implants, $400 cell phones, $10,000 watches, and the like. (Of course, not to be confused with *Sacraments*, which are something else altogether.)

**Security,** *noun.* Something traded on the Stock Exchange. There is no longer any other usage for this word since, by the grace of Our Father and Free Market Capitalism, people no longer have any other form of *Security*.

194

**Self,** *noun.*   The true center of the only religion worth the trouble.

**Self-Control,** *noun.*   Exceedingly difficult and not worth the trouble.

**Self-Knowledge,** *noun.*   Exceedingly difficult and not worth the trouble.

**Self-Mastery,** *noun.*   Exceedingly difficult and not worth the trouble.

**Self-Minded,** *adjective.*   High minded.

**Self-Occupied,** *adjective.*   Being devoted to a good cause.

**Self-Satisfied,** *noun.*   Having received the best satisfaction there is.

**Self-Serving,** *adjective.*   Receiving first class service.

**Selfishness,** *noun.* Is next to Godliness.


**Semester,** *noun.* The normal length of time (12 to 16 weeks) allowed for any college course or college romance, and between 4 and 6 per semester is the normal load.


**Sermon,** *noun.* A speech, always too long, that you don't need to listen to.


**Serpent,** *noun.* The king of the jungle, unfairly maligned in the Book of Genesis.


**Seven Cardinal Virtues**, *proper noun.* They are: wrath, greed, sloth, pride, lust, envy, and gluttony. But the greatest of these is pride.


**Sex,** *noun.* A purely recreational activity involving the genitals of one or any number of males and/or females and/or transgender people in the same room or in communication with each other by electronic means in real or virtual time. All sexual activity of any sort is strongly and unreservedly encouraged, except that which is allowed to result in the procreation of the human species.

**Sexist,** *noun & adjective.* Some one who is insensitive enough to think that there are such things as differences between the sexes; displaying the personality flaw that indicates one recognizes differences between the sexes and believes there may actually be personality traits linked to gender identity and/or sexual orientation.

**Sex Education,** *noun.* Instruction to youth in schools about sexual activity, sexual orientation, sexually transmitted disease, and sexual discrimination, as well as instruction in how to circumvent (physically and psychologically) the natural connection between sex and the procreation of the species. *Sex Education* in many Western societies has been highly successful in increasing sexual activity while decreasing procreation, and has been so very effective in Western European countries that most of their populations are happily no longer replacing themselves. (See *Birth Rate* and *Birth Control* and *Sexual Reproduction.*)

**Sex Industry,** *noun.* The world's oldest profession and the only industry that has never needed affirmative action to level the playing field. Our Father Below has always been and will continue to be an Equal Opportunity employer.

**Sex Scandal,** *noun.* All scandal is good but *Sex Scandal* is best.

**Sexual Appetite,** *noun.* Infinite and expanding, like the universe itself. Humans are the only mammals that can and do desire to have sexual intercourse 365 days a year, unless they are married.

**Sexual Harassment,** *noun and legal term.* Any unwanted form of human interaction, communication, and/or contact that might potentially have sexual overtones of any sort, intended or unintended, including but not limited to any of the following actions, if they are perceived by the aggrieved party to have been done in an improper and unwanted way: touching, talking, joking, listening, writing, looking, glancing, gesturing, breathing, smelling, sitting, eating, drinking, smoking, praying, partying, bike riding, farting, running, walking, working, swimming, shopping, teaching, scratching, burping, reading, and/or thinking. The foregoing applies to *Sexual Harassment* when the aggrieved party is female. When the aggrieved party is male, *Sexual Harassment* is considered to be harmless flirtation and is therefore not actionable in a court of law.

**Sexual Identity,** *noun.* We thought we knew, but now we know better.

**Sexual Mores,** *noun.* The word *Mores* comes from the plural of the Latin word *mos,* meaning custom or usage. *Mores* refers to agreed upon standards of behavior and attitude regarding matters of central importance that embody the fundamental moral views of a society. The term *Sexual Mores* no longer has any agreed upon meaning for people in First World societies because, quite simply, people no longer agree upon any sexual standards of behavior or attitude. Morality and *Mores* are now determined by vote, and some issues seem always to culminate in an irreducible plurality. This is the sublime beauty of *Pluralism* and *Relativism.*

**Sexual Politics,** *noun.* As if plain old politics wasn't bad enough.

**Sexual Reproduction,** *noun, biological term.* The form of biological procreation that depends upon the union of gametes. Gametes are the mature sexual reproduction cells, sperms and eggs. "Gamete" comes from the Greek words *gamete,* wife, and *gametes,* husband. (Note: perhaps this has something to do with the definition of the word *marriage* being a union between a husband and a wife.) All higher life forms, without exception, procreate themselves through *Sexual Reproduction.* With the arrival of the third millennium some humans have come to think that perhaps there's a way around the inconvenient dilemma of *Sexual Reproduction.* Well, we say more power to them and good luck with that. (See *Same Sex Marriage.*)

**Sexual Revolution,** *noun.* A period of time in the Western World during the 1960s & 70s and roughly contemporaneous with the arrival of the birth control pill for women. The *Sexual Revolution* brought about the happy result that millions upon millions of people in the First World were finally freed from the natural connection of sex to procreation, and thereby they became free to make sex into a recreational activity that now delightfully occupies more and more and more of their waking (and sleeping) hours. At the same time, the *Sexual Revolution* has brought forth a healthy, vital, and vigorous torrent of pornography, streaming its life giving waters across all classes and age groups of enlightened societies. Even more impressive than all of the above, the *Sexual Revolution* has also led to a decline in the First World's birth rate that is so severe it threatens to destroy the social contract between the generations. This is all good stuff. (See *Revolution.*)

**Shake-Spear, William,** *proper noun/name.* Pen name taken by Edward DeVere, the 17th Earl of Oxford.

**Shaksper, William,** *proper noun/name.* An illiterate grain merchant from Stratford, England, believed as an article of holy faith by many tenured professors to be the author known as *William Shake-Speare* or *William Shakespeare.*

**Shaman,** *noun.*   A professor of "Consciousness Studies," found at a growing number of small, trendy liberal arts colleges in the United States.

**Shame,** *noun.*   Something it's always best to be without.

**Sheep's Clothing,** *noun.*   Always the best choice for a well dressed wolf.

**The Silent Majority,** *collective noun.*   Our Father's loyal, if unwitting, assistants.

**Silicone,** *noun.*   A polymer that is fluid, resinous, rubbery, pliable, soft to the touch, and highly stable. There are many deposits in Los Angeles and Miami.

**Sin,** *verb & noun.*   To take any action, as comes naturally, to cause harm or insult to others, oneself, or one's God.   However, in the current highly psychoanalyzed Secular Age this word has ceased to have any clear meaning, and consequently it is no longer in use. All enlightened people know that *Sin* is merely an understandable, negative outcome/ symptom, caused by prior negative input ex-perience, which was thrust upon one by events outside of one's control.

**666,** *proper noun, name.* The Mark of the Blessed, the stigmata of Our Father Below. Originally, in the Book of Revelation, *666* was a numerical cryptogram for the illustrious Emperor Domitian, declared immortal by himself and the senate of Rome during his lifetime—an emperor who did his very best to prevent the world from being overrun by Christians.

**Slander,** *noun & verb.* To err is merely human, to *Slander* is devilishly divine.

**Social Contract,** *noun.* Don't worry about it—nothing but an antiquated idea that's not worth the paper it's not printed on. The free market and corporations will take care of everybody just fine.

**Social Darwinism,** *noun.* The well founded science which holds that not only are humans the direct and close descendants of beasts, which is manifestly obvious, but also that beasts in bloody competition with each other up and down the food chain provide us with the best role models for human behavior and social organization. (See *Competition, Darwinism* and *Evolution.*)

**Socrates,** *proper noun.* An ancient Greek philosopher (sophist) who lived in Athens c. 469-

399 B. C. He held informal meetings for young Athenians in various places, including a public grove known as the *Academe,* during which meetings he asked the unfortunate adolescents leading questions designed to confuse and confound them. Demonstrating good sense, the citizens of Athens condemned Socrates to death for corrupting their youth and promoting subversive ideas counter to the well being of the Athenian state.    (See *Academe, Academic Institution, Sophistry.*)


**Socratic Method,** *proper noun.*    A method of teaching, modeled after the style of Socrates, whereby the teacher asks a series of more and more confounding questions of the students, resulting in their becoming challenged, confused, disturbed, and distraught—and therefore more likely to be seduced by the subversive ideas the teacher wishes to inculcate and promote.  Socrates was condemned to death for his offense; college professors who today employ the *Socratic Method* are usually denied tenure and barely escape being condemned to death themselves.


**Sodom, Sodomy, Sodomite,** *proper noun.* *Sodomy* and *Sodomite* are inadmissible, offensive, and politically incorrect terms for an act or a person illegally discriminated against. These words all derive from the Bible in the *Book Of Genesis,* wherein the story is recounted of God's wrathful, impulsive, and vindictive annihilation of the town of *Sodom* because of the purported wickedness of its male citizens—i.e., their habit of men having sex with men as if they were women, something which the Old Testament God unequivocally prohibited and Christian teaching also insensitively condemned as being contrary to divine and natural law. This demonstrates the sad but unavoidable truth that God's old and new covenants do not seem to include the now standard civil rights clause establishing non-discrimination based on race, color, religious creed, ancestry, national origin, age, pregnancy, marital or parental status, disability, gender identity, or sexual orientation. This is one of the many reasons why God has been declared dead and is no longer an acceptable topic in polite society. (See *Friedrich Nietzsche* and *Investment Banker.*)

*Sola Scriptura (by Scripture alone),* *religious, theological phrase.* This is a religious term (well known in Latin and English) for the powerful Protestant concept that all that's necessary to be an upright Christian is to read and interpret Holy Scripture on one's own. According to this tenet, individual Christians do not need the assistance or mediation of any Church or priest to muddle up their reading of the Bible. Of course, this can and does lead to a myriad of different and conflicting interpretations—and that is why Our Father heartily approves of *Sola Scriptura.* Chaos is always good.

**Solidarity (Human Solidarity),** *proper noun.* A concept in Catholic Social Doctrine that refers to a divine demand placed upon all humans to respect and support each other in friendship, social charity, and brotherhood. Our Father Below has phrased a similar but different concept as, "Either all stand together or all be damned together separately." Fortunately for The Cause, rampant, virulent, and ever growing Individualism and Competition are providing a welcome counterforce to *Solidarity.* (See *Competition* and *Universal Brotherhood.*)

**Sophistry,** *noun.* The final stage of all philosophy.

**Sorrow,** *noun.* Yes, Oscar, where there is *Sorrow,* there is holy ground. *Sorrow* commemorates that what is lost is gone forever—and through this *Sorrow* one can sense the presence of a soul.

**Soul,** *noun.* 1) something African Americans have; 2) a type of music created by African Americans; 3) something White people in America sold a long time ago and they now rent from Black people. (See *Human Soul.*)

**Southern Baptist Convention,** *proper noun.* An annual convention of independent, passionate church congregations in the Southern United States, serving The Enemy with perhaps too much passion for their own good.

**Speaking in Tongues,** *verb.* 1) What a certain, but ever growing, percentage of New York City taxi drivers do when the uninitiated enter their cabs. 2) What a certain, but ever growing, percentage of Evangelical Christians do when entering their churches.

**Spin,** *noun.* Late 20$^{th}$ century word used to replace the word *truth*.

**Spirit, Holy Spirit,** *noun.* These words have no place in contemporary discourse, because it has been amply proven by empirical science that humans live in a material world devoid of *Spirit,* where everything has a material cause that is both necessary and sufficient. There is only life, which has accidentally arisen from random mutations in the material world; there is no "life of the spirit" either in the material or in the so-called immaterial world. Consequently, since there is no *Spirit,* there is no *Holy Spirit.*

**Spiritual,** *adjective.* The above notwithstanding, the Post-Modern world is surprisingly well stocked with those who declare themselves to be *Spiritual.* As in, for example: "I'm very *Spiritual*, I'm just not religious." From these speakers' perspective there is no contradiction, since *Spirit* is something personal that they have created and fostered in private on their own time and for their own purposes. As long as nothing about one's *Spirit* has anything to do with God, it is intellectually acceptable and politically correct in polite society to be just as *Spiritual* as one wants.

**Spurious,** *adjective.* The most valuable, useful, and important type of comments because they are never genuine, authentic, or true.

**Spurious Argument,** *noun.* Always the best argument to make.

**Spy,** *noun.* Some one who is unusually good at minding other people's business, unless he or she is employed by the C.I.A. (See *C.I.A.*)

**STD, Sexually Transmitted Disease,** *noun.* Solid proof that it's not necessarily better to give than to receive—Christian counsel to the contrary.

**Statistician, Statistics,** *noun.* Some one who manipulates numbers to fit any preconceived conclusion that may be required. There are two kinds of *Statistics*: damn *Statistics* and God damned *Statistics*. The same for *Statisticians,* and we ought to know because—if we may employ a particularly apt metaphor from the *Book of Genesis*—the apples don't fall far from the tree. (See *Poll.*)

**Steady State, Steady State Theory,** *proper noun.* The *Steady State Theory* of the universe was the atheist's best friend—for a little while, between 1948 till the late 1960's—but then the discovery of the Big Bang's cosmic microwave background radiation blew *Steady State* right out of the water. The *Steady State Theory* was an attempt to preserve the Eternal Return model of the universe—that is, the old *pre*-Judeo-Christian idea that the universe has always been here forever and will always remain, perhaps engaging in certain cycles, but always existing in a steady state, sustaining itself with no beginning and no ending. *Steady State* was the atheist's friend because, if the universe has always been here and always just goes on, then (presto!) there is no annoying question about a First Cause, or a Creator, or an Initial Singularity, or anything outside of time and space. But there was a major glitch: the *Steady State Theory* just didn't hold up to observation and experiment. Astronomy, astro-physics, and subatomic physics all prove that there was a beginning, and the data show that the beginning was about 15 billion years ago. The First Cause is now called *The Initial Singularity,* and this Singularity is pretty damn near the same thing as God the Creator. Heck, even our Father Below has to admit it: Just call a spade a spade, for God's sake! Or should we say for *Singularity's* sake?

**A Stitch in Time,** *colloquial expression.* Is usually not worth the trouble.

**Stock Exchange,** *noun.* An international charitable institution to provide and care for stock brokers and investment bankers.

**Stoned,** *adjective.* 1) Being pleasantly high from smoking weed in the Christian world; 2) being severely beaten by rocks as a punishment in the Muslim world. There appears to be some distance to go before finding common ground.

**Subvert, Subversion,** *verb, noun.* From the Latin *sub* (below) + *vetere* (to turn). To overturn something or turn something over so that what was (unfairly) below is then on top. *Subversion* is the greatest weapon against those (or Him) on top.

**Suicide,** *noun.* A graceful exit.

**Suck,** *verb.* 1) To draw into the mouth by action of the lips and tongue, thereby producing a partial vacuum. 2) Colloquial, to fail miserably or to be unpleasant. 3) The sound made by jobs and capital leaving a country due to the joys of Globalization.

**ior Race,** *noun.* Usually the white one, but cally any race, as long as the speaker considers himself a member of it.

**Supreme Court,** *proper noun.* An appointed body in Washington, used by Republicans to unethically sway elections in their favor, used by Democrats to unethically sway legislation in their favor, and used by *Supreme Court* members to legislate from the bench, thereby avoiding the cumbersome process of legislating through the legislature.

**Surrogate Mother,** *noun.* A woman who willingly provides (usually for a fee) her womb to give birth to an embryo obtained from another source. The embryo may be obtained in a number of different ways: a) from another couple; b) from one of the couple's eggs or sperm combined with an anonymous egg or sperm; or c) from the combination of anonymous eggs and anonymous sperm. The child born of this process has a birth certificate not bearing the *Surrogate Mother's* name; the parent (or parents) on the birth certificate are those in the contractor position—i.e., whoever contracted with the *Surrogate Mother* to arrange for the birth. In this contractual arrangement all parties' rights are carefully protected—except the right of the child to have and to know its biological parents.

**Switzerland,** *proper noun.* A small, supposedly neutral country in Europe where Our Father does all his banking in secret, unidentifiable, tax free accounts.


**Sycophant,** *noun.* 1) A self-seeking, servile flatterer; 2) a fawning parasite; 3) a professional lobbyist; 3) an atheist with second thoughts on his deathbed.


**Synecdoche,** *noun.* The ancient name for a common rhetorical device in classical Greek and Latin oratory, whereby a figure of speech is created that uses a part of something in place of the whole, thereby achieving a desired effect. As in, for example: "Man, that guy is an asshole." A useful word to be used in polite society as follows: "Pardon my *Synecdoche*, but that guy is an asshole."

**Take,** *verb.* To obtain something by any means possible while making sure one has good legal representation.

**Talk,** *verb.* The action that precedes the verb *Take.*

**Talk Radio,** *noun.* Our Father's infernal Word made flesh.

**Taste,** *noun.* There's no accounting for it and we can thank our Father for that. (See *Relativism.*)

**Tattoo,** *noun and verb.* The very ancient art of puncturing the surface layer of the skin and placing pigments into it, thereby creating indelible designs, pictures, signs, or in modern times words that one later regrets. Originally used by humans to identify themselves as loyal members of a specific group or tribe, in modern times the *Tattoo* is used by struggling, economically disadvantaged youth for the same ancient tribal purpose—while it is used by comfortable, economically advantaged youth for exactly the opposite purpose. For females, having a *Tattoo* is now a requirement for admission to many New England colleges.


**Team,** *noun.* From the Old English word *Team*, meaning a set of draft-hauling animals. In modern English usage, the word *Team* refers to a group of humans behaving as if they were a set of draft-hauling animals.


**Team Player,** *noun.* Some one who puts the best interests of his *Team* ahead of his own and his society's best interests, while behaving like a draft-hauling animal.
(See *Yes Man.*)


**Team Sports,** *noun.* A method of training impressionable youth so that as they mature they will learn how to: 1) be submissive to the domination of their captain, their coach, or their Chief Executive Officer; 2) work together like a *Team* of draft-hauling animals; 3) beat others down while bending every rule of the game right up to its breaking point; and 4) become people who put the best interests of their *Team* ahead of their own and their society's best interests. Our Father's favorite *Team Sports* are the ones that also involve the most physical violence: football and hockey lead the list. How can anyone possibly question the benefits to mankind of school and professional *Team Sports?*

Any activity that brings humans closer to behaving like animals is always a good thing.

**Television,** *noun.*   The primary means of Sacred Teaching employed by Our Father Below in his daily instruction to the world.

**Temperance,** *noun.*   A word that has fallen out of common usage; few know what it used to mean and no one knows what it might mean today. *Q.E.D.*

**Tempt,** *verb.*   Deuteronomy 6:16 notwithstanding, You shall *Tempt* the Lord your God. What on earth else are you here for?

**Temple Mount**, *proper noun.*   A small piece of land raised above the old city of Jerusalem that is a sacred site for Jews, Christians, and Muslims. It is the most contested parcel of real estate on the planet; the sequence of title is a glorious mess. There's nothing like a good fight between the world's three monotheisms to bring out the best in people.

**Temptation,** *noun.*   The root of all virtue.

**The Ten Infernal Commandments**, *proper noun.*
They are: 1) Thou shalt have as many gods as thou
wantest as they are all pathways to the True Cause;
2) Idols are just as good as gods; 3) Thou shalt
blaspheme regularly as it is good for the soul; 4)
Thou shalt remember the Sabbath as the best sales
are usually held on that day; 5) Place thy father and
thy mother in an old age home as quickly as
possible after receiving power of attorney; 6) Thou
shalt not murder unless it is for something really
important; 7) A little adultery is good for any
marriage; 8) Stealing is the name of the game, but
if Thou stealest on too small a scale thou mayest
end up in jail, so thou must steal on a truly grand
scale, join the right clubs, and then thy government
will have to bail thee out; 9) Bearing false witness
is the only way to make justice work for thee; 10)
Covet thy neighbor's wife since she is probably in a
bad marriage anyway and looking to do
commandment number seven. (Note: Not to be
confused with *The Ten Commandments*.)

**Terrorism**, *noun.* A superior form of warfare by
which civilians are consistently killed in more
numbers than fighters in or out of uniform. Note:
*Terrorism* is always and only committed by those
on the opposite side from the speaker.

**Testify**, *verb.* Closely related to the Latin word for
testicle, *testis/testes.* But the fainthearted insist that
the root is from the Latin word for "third", even

though there is a mountain of evidence, especially in the Old Testament, that men had to *Testify* by placing their hand on their testicles. A testicle was proof of maleness, and maleness was required for "testimony." So here we have the original form of swearing to tell the truth being based on having the balls to tell the truth. *Q. E. D.*

**Testosterone,** *noun.* The male steroid sex hormone, now illegal in many First World countries.

**Theater of the Absurd,** *noun, literary term.* Realistic drama.

**Theism,** *proper noun.* The belief that there is a God or Gods somewhere, and he, she, it or they do influence the course of the universe, but mankind doesn't know what to call it or them and doesn't understand it or them—likewise, it or they don't seem to understand mankind either and perhaps have no interest or capacity to do so. If this sounds like a damn fine pickle to be stuck in, that's because it would be if it were true. But Our Father Below advises mankind to take heart because: the good news is *Deism* and *Theism* have got it all wrong, and the bad news is *Deism* and *Theism* have got it all wrong. The Enemy hasn't left and he hasn't lost interest. (See *Deism.*)

**Theologian,** *noun.* An accountant who works for the Enemy, counting imaginary angels sitting on the heads of real pins; although, we have reason to know, some of them now serve Our Father Below—whether they know it or not.

**Third World,** *proper noun.* The place where the people of the First World have assigned all the other people on earth to live.

**Time,** *noun.* Is the most valuable thing to waste.

**Tomorrow,** *noun.* The day after today, always the best day to begin reform; never reform a vice today that could just as well be reformed tomorrow.

**Torture,** *noun & verb.* What the other side, opposite from the speaker, does to obtain information from captured enemy combatants, from those who assist enemy combatants, from those who are related to enemy combatants, and/or from those who look like enemy combatants. The speaker's side only interrogates to obtain information.

**Tragedy,** *noun.* 1) Any life altering event, and there are usually several in everyone's life, when you just don't realize the joke's on you—or, if you do, you don't appreciate the humor.    2) In the theater, a form of Realism.

**Tragic-Comedy,** *literary term.*    A realistic play.

**Tragic Flaw,** *noun.*    Something a literary hero has, but a Secular Humanist reader never has.

**Transcend, Transcendence,** *verb & noun.*    A religious and philosophical term that is indirectly derived from the verb "*descend*," with the suffix mistakenly changed to *trans-* by a fatigued (and probably drunk) medieval monastic scribe.    One cannot *trans*cend, one can only *de*scend—after all, gravity is a universal force of nature.

**Transgender,** *noun & adjective.*    This is a new word created by those who either:   a) change their gender through surgery and hormonal treatments; b) object to society's restrictive and discriminatory definitions of gender; and/or 3) consider themselves separate from, above and beyond any known definition of gender.    Somewhat like a Trans-national Corporation (see entry below), being *Transgender* is the best way to do whatever one wants by placing oneself separate from, above and beyond any gender's sovereignty.    And, after all, being beyond any and all sovereignty is always the best way to be.

**Transnational Corporation,** *noun.* See entry for *Corporation* and then multiply it by a factor of 100. The best way for a corporation to do whatever it wants is to place itself separate from, above and beyond any nation's sovereignty. And, after all, being beyond any and all sovereignty is always the best way to be. (See *Transgender.*)

**Transubstantiation (Real Presence),** *noun.* A controversial theological term used in the Catholic Church to refer to the actual, *Real Presence* of the body and blood of Jesus Christ that (purportedly) miraculously appears (*Transubstantiates)* in the bread and wine upon its consecration by a Catholic priest during the mass. This straining of credulity is neither necessary nor asked for by Protestant denominations, since they make no claim that Christ has a *Real Presence* in their sanctuaries. Similarly, they have taken Christ off the cross: that is, they display a bare cross only, never a crucifix, in their churches. Protestants politely consider this *Transubstantiation & Real Presence* thing a minor detail, but Catholics politely disagree. Well, it hasn't always been polite—actually over the last 400 years this disagreement has caused the deaths of thousands. Our Father Below heartily approves.

**Trash,** *noun.* Another man's treasure.

**Trophy Wife,** *noun.* A social institution of ancient pedigree and good sense. After a man has worked hard, won at the game, screwed over his competitors, employees and partners, as well as divorced his first wife (or second or third), he is surely entitled to a nice trophy in this life for his steadfast efforts. After all, he won't be getting any rewards for his efforts in the next life.

**Truth,** *noun.* A word no longer in current use. (See *Post-Modernism,* and *Spin.*)

**Truths,** *noun.* The above entry notwithstanding, our brother Nietzsche has said: All *Truths* that are kept silent become poisonous.

**Two-Party System,** *noun.* A one-party political system with two halves for the haves, and no half for the have-nots.

# U

**Ubermench, Super-man**, *proper noun.* The True Destiny of man, from beast to human to Super-man, as per the theology of brother Friedrich Nietzsche. It is the divinely ordained fate of man to cease to exist in order that he may be replaced by the Super-man who will live by the Will to Power and be beyond good and evil.

**Ultimatum,** *noun.* The final demand before giving in to the lesser of two evils.

**Unbiased Opinion,** *noun, oxymoron.* There is no such thing—merely a figment of the imagination.

**Uncertain,** *adjective.* Unfortunately, it is not certain that everything is *Uncertain.*

**Unconventional Warfare,** noun. The opposite of conventional warfare. Instead of striving to achieve victory through the use of straight forward military might and the infliction of death and destruction upon the enemy's armies, *Unconventional Warfare* is striving to achieve victory through the use of any and all clandestine means—including but not limited to subversion, intimidation, bribery, blackmail, blockades, sanctions, character assassination, actual assassination, military coups, kidnapping, and terrorism. Our Father Below did not think it was possible to improve upon conventional warfare, but mankind continues to accomplish the impossible.

**Underage,** *adjective.* Depends on the state and country. More and more fashion models look fourteen years old, so culturally speaking *Underage* is harder and harder to define. Good things come to those who wait. (See *Lolita.*)

**Ungodly / Godless,** *adjective.* There is a subtle yet crucial distinction here, for example: a *Godless Age* is a time that has no God and also denies that God exists; whereas an *Ungodly Age* is a time that does not deny God exists, but instead refuses to acknowledge God exists and refuses to act as if God exists. The act of refusal is crucial. Our Father always prefers, with good reason, the *Ungodly* to the *Godless.*

**Unitarian Universalist,** *proper noun.* Some sort of religion. We have no idea what. . . and neither do they.

**Universal Brotherhood (***aka* **Solidarity),** *term of Catholic Social Doctrine.* This is the pernicious concept and principle that all of humanity is closely related, is in effect one great family, and for this reason all humans have both a divine and biological command to treat each other with brotherly love, understanding, and charity. Unfortunately, late 20$^{th}$ century developments in genetic anthropology have confirmed that all humans are indeed closely related to each other and that everyone around the world is descended from a tiny group of wanders who walked out of Africa in a north-northeasterly direction about 50,000 years ago. Fortunately, many world leaders remain unimpressed by either the theological or the anthropological argument, so the infernal fratricide continues unabated.

**United Nations,** *proper noun.* There's precious little united about them. We rest our case. *Q.E.D.*

**Upper Class,** *noun.* The class that thought up the term *Lower Class.*

**V,** *letter, symbol.*   Is for victory!   At all costs.

**Wall Street,** *proper noun.*    A street in lower Manhattan that was the location of a wall built by America's settlers to protect themselves from the rest of the island's population (i.e., the other people who lived there first and used to own it).  Today it is a street in lower Manhattan that is the location of a wall built by America's brokerage houses to protect themselves from the rest of the country's population (i.e., the other people who lived there first and used to own it).

**Wall Street Journal,** *proper noun/name.*    A daily newspaper that prints all the news that fits the needs of Free Market Republicans. (See *New York Times.)*

**War,** *noun.*   The most sublime activity of man, the action that gives him meaning.

**War Crimes,** *noun & legal concept.*    A contradiction in terms:  All's fair in love and war.

**War on Terror,** *noun, political term.* An oxymoron of deadly accuracy.

**War is Hell,** *colloquial expression.* Yes, indeed, and how sweet it is.

**WASP,** *proper noun.* An acronym formed from the words White, Anglo-Saxon, and Protestant. A sociological-religious term for a group of people in the United States who consider themselves to be the country's only true Native American bipeds without feathers, melanin, or crucifixes. This group has always been open and accepting of members from all American Christian groups except Catholics, who are not welcome and need not apply. (See *Militia Movement.*)

**Weak,** *adjective.* The natural condition of man, ensuring that he will always tend to fulfill Our Father's Plan.

**Weapons of Mass Destruction,** *noun.* Always good to have around, even if you can't find them when you most need to find them—e.g., in Iraq. (See *Defense Contractor.*)

**Whimper,** *verb & noun.* To cry with a low, plaintive, broken sound. And as Old Possum said it ﹐so very well, "This is the way the world ends . . . not with a bang but with a *Whimper.*"

**White,** *noun & adjective.* A shade of gray.

**White Collar Crime,** *noun.* Business as usual on Wall Street; organized crime in the right zip code.

**White Race,** *noun.* The superior one, at least according to them. For our part, Our Father Below doesn't know what the *White Race* is, or even what *Race* is. But since it causes a fight, all's for the best.

**Wisdom of Solomon,** *proper noun.* If Solomon was so wise, then why is his book only in the Apocrypha and not in the real Bible?

**Wicca,** *proper noun.* A growing *neo-pagan* religion made popular in the 1950s by a retired and highly eccentric British civil servant named Gerald Gardner. It has matured into a 21st century religion tailored to witchcraft and witches, highly popular among the dread-locked, white, middle class, female, neo-hippy set native to small New England colleges. To date, none of the *nouveau* witches on

New England's campuses have been executed—however, all should remember with caution that the infamous Salem Witch Trials did take place in New England.  But, one sincerely hopes, with the growing momentum of politically correct religious tolerance we can rest assured that the civil rights of these new *Wicca* witches will not be violated, up to and including their sacred right to sacrifice chickens, goats, and young boys.


**Willing Suspension of Disbelief,** *noun, literary concept.*  Something one needs to get through reading a novel or to get through living in the real world.


**Wisdom,** *noun.*  That rarefied stage of intellectual development, rarely attained by humans (and never by professors), when one realizes that one has learned and understood nothing, and that all one's efforts have brought one no closer to learning or understanding anything.


**Witch,** *noun.*  Tragically, in the old days a woman or girl convicted of being a witch used to be burned at the stake.  In the late 20$^{th}$ century things greatly improved and now witches have their own religion and are guaranteed their religious freedom like everyone else.  Who says there's no such thing as progress?  (See *Wicca.*)

**Women's Rights,** *noun & legal term.* The term *Women's Rights* represents an ever growing group of rights formerly held by men. There is no corresponding term *"Men's Rights"* because men do not have rights; men have advantages and privileges, which they regularly abuse. (See *Sexual Harassment.*)

**World Bank, International Monetary Fund, World Trade Organization,** *nouns.* Male fraternal organizations founded after World War II to keep the reins of Western economic power tightly in the grip of men (and we do mean men) whose native language is English.

**Writer,** *noun.* Some one, as Samuel Becket said, who is afflicted with a compulsion to say something and to find the words to say it, when there is nothing to say and no way to say it.

**Writing,** *noun.* Is something like sex, as brother Moliere said, first you do it for love, then you do it for a few friends, and finally you do it for money.

# X

**X,** *rating symbol.* A mark that used to be reserved for only the best movies.

**Xe Services LLC,** *proper noun/name.* New name for the most successful, yet most controversial, private mercenary corporation in the world, formerly known as *Blackwater USA* and then *Blackwater Worldwide;* a name change was necessitated by bad press received regarding the company's noble efforts in Iraq. The new name was chosen because no one will ever remember how to spell, or ever be able to pronounce, *"Xe"* and therefore the company will be less likely to receive bad press in the future. The *"LLC"* in the company's name stands for "Limited Liability Corporation" and if anyone ever needed the legal protection of *Limited Liability* these guys do. Thank goodness (or something else) for the corporate lawyers and spin doctors of America who have made these great efforts possible.

**Xmas,** *proper noun.* The politically correct way to write the word *Christmas*, thereby leaving Christ out of Christmas. Or, in some circles, a way to write the word Christmas that is offensive because the "X" symbol is understood as equal to the advertising industry's use of "Brand X" for the name of an inferior competitor. However, it must be noted, that both of these uses are due to extreme ignorance. The symbol *"X"*, indicating the word *Christ*, has a history going back almost 2,000 years. It comes from the first letter of the word for *Christ* in Greek (*Xristos*), being the Greek translation of the Hebrew word *Masiah (Messiah)*, which means *The Anointed One*. Hence, *Jesus Christ* means *Jesus the Anointed One*. For Our Cause, it is heartening news that this sacred meaning of *"X"* has been almost completely forgotten and eradicated. Progress comes in small steps at a time.

**Year,** *noun.* A period of 365 wasted days and failures.

**Yes Man**, *noun.* A Devil's Disciple. (See *Team Player*.)

**Yesterday,** *noun.* The day before today, when everything was always better. (See *Second Law of Thermodynamics)*

**YHWH,** *proper noun.* The Enemy. Spelled without vowels in Biblical Hebrew.

**You,** *pronoun.* The least important word in the English Language. (See *I* )

**Your Word,** *noun.* As Napoleon said: The best way to keep *Your Word* is never to give it.

**Youth,** *noun.*  That blessed stage of man when he knows the most about everything and has the most potential for every evil—it should never be wasted.

# Z

**Zarathustra,** *proper noun/name.* The central figure of the sacred text *Thus Spoke Zarathustra* by brother Freidrich Neitzsche. The True Chosen One, Son of Our Father Below, the Word of Eternal Darkness, and perhaps even the Anti-Christ. No one enters the Kingdom Below except through him. **OF COURSE, ZARA-THUSTRA, SATAN, LUCIFER, THE DEVIL AND HELL ARE ALL FICTIONAL, SO MANKIND REALLY HAS NOTHING TO WORRY ABOUT.** Relax.

\*     \*     \*

# FINIS.
(The end)

# POX VOBISCUM.
(A pox be with you.)

\*     \*     \*

Made in the USA
Las Vegas, NV
04 February 2022

43149072R00139